T0129706

FOCUS TO PASS

FOCUS TO PASS

Success Guide for International Students

Felix Eshesimua

FOCUS TO PASS
SUCCESS GUIDE FOR INTERNATIONAL STUDENTS

iUniverse books may be ordered through booksellers or by contacting:

iUniverse
1663 Liberty Drive
Bloomington, IN 47403
www.iuniverse.com
1-800-Authors (1-800-288-4677)

Because of the dynamic nature of the Internet, any web addresses or links contained in this book may have changed since publication and may no longer be valid. The views expressed in this work are solely those of the author and do not necessarily reflect the views of the publisher, and the publisher hereby disclaims any responsibility for them.

Any people depicted in stock imagery provided by Getty Images are models, and such images are being used for illustrative purposes only.
Certain stock imagery © Getty Images.

ISBN: 978-1-5320-6723-5 (sc)
ISBN: 978-1-5320-6724-2 (e)

Print information available on the last page.

iUniverse rev. date: 01/31/2019

Dedication

This book is dedicated to all international students, my family, my deceased father, and my newborn son. These people have been my motivation for all my accomplishments.

International students are the future and are the leaders of tomorrow. They are the pillars that will make the world a better place. As an international student myself, I know the focus and vision of all international students so, I am dedicating this book to international students all over the world.

International students have added to the global GDP and they are constantly growing our global economy. We have already started making change and adding value to the world in IT, healthcare, manufacturing, educational development, engineering, just to name a few.

I also have a vision that one day, very soon, the world will have peace, there will be no killings, not tribal or religious wars – a world where everyone treats others equally, regardless of race, color, sex, or tribe.

Felix Eshesimua

The FOCUS Strategy for Student Success

In this success guide, you will learn about the **FOCUS strategy** to help you to achieve your best potential and to succeed as an international student.

I have identified the most important factors in student success. I refer to these factors as **FOCUS**, which includes 5 success actions that can fuel your success. They are:

1. **F**ocus on graduation.
2. **O**vercome stress and challenges.
3. **C**ommunicate your feelings regardless of the opinion of others.
4. **U**nderstand your strengths and weaknesses.
5. **S**tudy your environment, your people, and your world.

This success guide explains these 5 important factors that will help you to achieve your full potential. There are sections where you can take notes and record your thoughts and ideas after reviewing each chapter. International student success features are also included to inspire you with stories from students just like you.

So, get ready to **FOCUS** and become the success that you are destined to be.

Notes

What do you hope to learn from this book?
What are you struggling with as an international student?
What support do you need to succeed as a student?
What is causing you stress and anxiety?
What are your goals, before and after graduation?

Contents

CHAPTER 1

Focus on Graduation

*"Human progress is neither automatic nor inevitable...
Every step toward the goal of justice requires sacrifice, suffering, and struggle;
the tireless exertions and passionate concern of dedicated individuals."*
- Martin Luther King, Jr.

It was August 2007, the first time I came to the United States of America. I was very excited because after all my sleepless nights of continuously studying for the SAT and the TOEFL, my dreams came true. My long-term dream of studying in the United States didn't yet become a reality when I was at the Airport and on the plane, during layovers and transfers. I still couldn't believe I was traveling abroad to the United States of America "God's own country" as many young and smart West African students refer to the dream of coming to the U.S. It wasn't until my plane landed in Pittsburgh, PA, that I felt this undeniable joy coming right from my soul, as if the angels just opened the doors to heaven.

While fasting and praying endlessly with hope to get my student visa approved, I promised God that I would always live to glorify his name. So, the first thing I did when I arrived in the U.S., with tears slowing falling from my eyes, was give thanks to the most high for my new home.

A woman was already at the airport waiting for me. Her name was Daniella, my cousin Abraham's girlfriend at the time. Now they're married with kids. Daniella was a very sweet lady just like those I had seen in American romance movies. She was very calm, lovely, and approachable.

She welcomed me with a great heart. When we were driving to their apartment, she asked me about my trip and life in West Africa. I remember being distracted from the conversation, as I was very busy looking at the roads, buildings, and people. I was very fascinated by everything I saw. It was amazing to me, just like I had pictured it.

Focus Fact:
Every international student undeniably
gets great chills when they land in America.
It's like that WOW/DAMN! feeling!

Pardon me for deviating with my first experience coming to America. I will save that part for one of my future books or I'll post an article at Itoto House about the experience! For this book, I will dive into the reason why focusing on graduation is very important, to becoming a successful international student.

Did you know that statistics indicate that 6 out of 10 students that enter the United States with a student visa end up dropping out of school, getting married, going back home, living in the street, ending up in jail, or getting deported? That means that only 40% of international students that come to the U.S. to follow their dreams, actually achieve them. Yes, it's true according to: SmartCollege Visit.[1]

I almost became one of those people. But the Power of FOCUS kept me going and I never stopped pushing and fighting the tough transition. There were instances when I struggled to get out of my cold and small dorm room bed. There were times when I couldn't understand my professors. There were even several days, when I felt so alone and wished I had a friend, family, or a community to turn to. But all of that seemed so far away. There were even times when some people made me feel unimportant and unwanted. But giving up was not an option.

---

[1] http://smartcollegevisit.com/2014/06/international-students-dropping-out-higher-numbers.html

I decided to break out of my comfort zone. It was a tough decision but I realized if I wanted to stay positive, if I wanted to graduate, if I wanted to make myself and my family proud, if I wanted to be competitive, if I wanted to prove to my parents that my decision was right for me, if I wanted to shame the devil, I needed to not only graduate but also help other people who faced the same challenges.

I needed to be part of school organizations, part of the community, interact with people, whether they understood my accent or not, whether they liked my skin color or not. I needed to ask questions in order to learn.

While trying to do all these things, my main goal and focus was on seeing myself graduate. Every time I got scared, nervous, felt lonely, missed home, missed my family, missed food I was used to, missed the weather I was used to, I just tuned my psychological button to graduation thoughts.

Let me briefly tell you about those graduation thoughts. They were happy and self-accomplishment thoughts. It was a thought that even if I was in excruciating pain, as soon as I remembered graduation, I easily forgot the pain. I could turn my tears to joy with my focus on graduation.

The first time I remember having to switch my mindset was in my English class when I raised my hand and asked a question about run-on sentences. The class started laughing even before I finished. I didn't know if they thought I was stupid, if my question was funny, if my words were funny, or if it was because of my accent. The professor did not understand me, so he couldn't answer my question. Instead of being sad, I slowly rephrased my question and he then got it and answered me. And I could tell from the silence of the class that they realized it was a great question and I believe one or more people that had the same question were glad I asked it.

But the point here is, if I wasn't able to switch my mindset at that point, I would not have gotten an answer to my question. I would have probably been sad the rest of the day and wouldn't be able to pay attention in my other classes.

Focus Fact:
Many international students cannot perform
to their fullest potential because of how
others see and judge them.

The second incident was at the library. This was an interesting situation. I needed help setting up my account to access the computers at the library, since I couldn't afford to have a personal laptop or desktop. So, I walked up to the desk to seek assistance from this beautiful young and charming lady. I can remember her beautiful demeanor. While walking toward her, she started smiling at me from afar. So, I had no option but to start smiling too. Before getting to the desk, I started practicing how to explain what I needed her assistance with. I wanted to speak clearly so she could understand me. But I got distracted by her obvious and continuous smile. Guess what happened, I messed it up. She had to bring in the manager to see if she could understand me better.

Now, I can laugh about it, but then it was like going for your first interview. I was so ashamed and embarrassed. During this process, I kept thinking how come they can't clearly understand me, but I can understand them. Because I was paying close attention and looking at their lips and reading them. I was so disappointed, I left the library that day without setting up my account and I got an F on the first assignment. I could have done or tried some other methods to make them help me that day like writing it on a piece of paper or being patient and trying a different tone. I went to my dorm that evening, frustrated.

But here is the good part, I ran into that same lady again while walking to class. It just so happened that we took the same route to the Hendrix building at Edinboro University. Her class was right next to mine. After walking and chatting on our way to class for a week, I started understanding her more and she seemed to start understanding me more. So, she gave me her work hours and said I should stop by when she was working, and she would help me. I stopped by the very next day and not only did she help me set up my account, we became very good friends. Never let one failed attempt stop you from trying again. Always look for different ways to solve a challenging channel of communication.

The third occasion that I applied the first tip to becoming a successful international student was during a chat with my dorm mate, Shawn. Shawn was a typical Caucasian man. He had never roomed with a black man all through his college career and it was his last semester as a Junior. He was very religious and straight forward. He asked me lots of questions about things that he never saw explained in the media or from his friends, or his parents.

At first, I thought Shawn just wanted to make fun of me. But as I got to know him better I got to understand he was trying to learn and get to know me better, rather than listening to the media. His first questions were to ask me if I wore nice clothing in Africa or did I just start wearing better clothes when I got to the states. I was like (*what the F?*). He kept trying to explain himself. "*Well that's what I was told and one time I saw on a documentary naked people in Africa.*" He made it seem funny, but it wasn't funny to me because I have never been naked in public, and I never saw naked people while growing up.

Me and Shawn had lots of culture-based Q&A. But this is what I learned from Shawn - always find out what other people know or don't know before making judgments - like the usual saying "*never judge a book by its cover.*"

One day Shawn and I decided to take a walk together, this was when it started getting cold toward the end of the fall semester. He said, "*Felix make sure you graduate and be the best in what you do because I believe you're going places and you will be a great black man.*" For a minute in my head I was like what do you mean? Black men are not great? He then went on further, "*Because black people my family knows never made it to college and the ones that did, never graduated, but I think you are a different black person.*"

Suddenly, it clicked in my head. NEVER GIVE UP. Since that day, I never missed one class except the days I was very sick and couldn't move.

I always switched the tone when I felt like not going to class. I hope you find that one thing that will always keep you pushing regardless of any struggles you face.

Focus Fact:
Many international students Judge others by their appearance.
Try to understand why they are asking negative questions.

The fourth time I had to switch on my tune, to focus on graduation, was toward the end of my Sophomore year. Now, I had a full-time job at the library. Don't ask me how but yes that beautiful smiling library lady helped make it happen, lol. I was a fast learner and good at paying attention to details, so I was already blending in. I could hold a conversation, people could understand me better, and I could understand people better. Although up until today, I still have an accent. Unlike many international students that do everything possible to speak 100% America English, I chose to keep my accent because it helps a lot during college and after college. I might tell you how in my next book or next two books or better still might reveal it at Itoto House. For those of you who haven't heard of Itoto House go check us out: **www.itoto.org** for international students. Make sure you register and follow us on social media, too.

Okay, let's get back to our focusing on graduation topic. Also, at this stage I was the V.P of International Students. I always knew I had the desire to help others grow and I decided to be part of the International Student organization, so I could motivate fellow international students to become successful on and off campus.

International night is an event the international students and the International Office put together yearly to showcase traditions, fashion, food from different countries, music, and talent shows. As the V.P/Host I was entitled to give a speech. I initially didn't have the time to give a speech, because I was busy planning and rehearsing for our performance.

During the networking/food section my favorite part, I got to chat with a much older man from West Africa who happened to be a dropout in the early 80s. He was married to a white woman and they had four kids.

Five minutes into our conversation, he introduced me to his family and by the time he was about to go to his table he held my hand and whispered to me, *"son, no matter what you do in college, always remember where you came from, always have it at the back of your mind you are a minority, you will have to do double what a typical indigene will do in order to succeed and be recognized. "Make Sure you graduate because nobody told me this."* He smiled and walked away. I couldn't stop thinking about it after the show and during my final speech to my team.

I had to share my own version of making sure you graduate with my team. And my speech was so powerful that this one student from Canada, that was already thinking of dropping out and going back home started crying. She said she couldn't stand the cold, laid back, and unwelcoming people and she was not doing well in her classes. But lo and behold she graduated - before me. I was her mentor despite the fact she was a year ahead of me. That's when I tuned up my volume of focusing on graduating.

My fifth tune up was during her graduation ceremony. It was the day Christine had been praying and hoping for the day she had always dreamed of, the day she had worked so hard for. The day her family was coming all the way from Canada to celebrate this great occasion with her. I could tell from her relieved smile she was ready to be done and eager for the next chapter of her life. At that point, I was a Junior although the fact that I still had one more year to go felt like 10 years to go.

Classes were becoming more challenging and working over 65 hours a week does not make it any better or easier. My wish was: oh, I wish I was graduating with Christine. That moment, I became down because I kept thinking of the next semester. I didn't even know if they would let me register for classes, as I still owed for the previous semester. I wasn't looking forward to taking another year off just to work and save money to get back to college. I felt I had already wasted so much time not being in school for one academic year because of owing the school money.

All these thoughts and many other thoughts kept going through my head, until the special guest, who happened to be an alumna, started giving his speech to the graduates. His stories were as if it was all for me. He kept talking about the struggle, stress, commitment, sacrifice, and hard work necessary to achieve results. He kept emphasizing the achievement would be like the daylight after a long dark night.

The achievement would bring great self-fulfillment and accomplishment. He mentioned that's when you feel like the doors of heaven have just been opened for you. At that point, I stared at Christine and her smile couldn't make me agree more. I told myself at that point I was going to do all it took to make sure I graduated the next year, do or die. I tuned up the volume key all the way to the max. I kept that mindset all year, while working, studying, going to class, meeting, having conversations, working out, eating, praying daily, and I dreaming about me working - so many times that it became real to me and nobody or no situation could convince me that I wouldn't graduate the next year.

Despite all that happened that year, 2014 and despite my dad passing three months before my graduation, I still graduated above average - although my GPA dropped drastically. That was the beginning of my problem, as it affected my life, and turned my life around. That is another topic for another day, I promise I will touch on it.

"Everything you need you already have;
you are complete right now.
You are a whole total person,
not an apprentice person on the way to someplace else.
Your completeness must be understood by you
and experienced in your thoughts
as your own personal reality."
- Wayne Dyer

Finally, have a game plan.
A great way to stay focused is developing and being able to be in the habit of staying focused. It sounds like one of those sayings that it is easier to say than do or accomplish, right? It's not exactly that but on the other hand, don't worry, it's doable. You just have to discover your potential, you have to know the things that make you or will make you jump out of bed at 5am every morning. This is especially if doing that for the rest of your life would mean doing everything you wanted or would love to do for the rest of your life. I am not talking about getting up early for Soccer, Football, or Lacrosse practice because your coach wants you to or because it is required for you to stay on the team. I am saying getting up early to do what you love.

Unfortunately, most of us don't like getting up early especially for classes. It makes it even worse when you have been up all night studying or rather hanging out with friends. Let me tell you this. If I was able to discover the importance of getting up from my bed at 5am every morning and it would be very rewarding and at least I would have mastered it by now.

I get up every day except the weekends at 5am to start my day and I absolutely love it. But I hated it back then in college. What I am trying to say here is that the earlier you discover the things, dreams, purpose, activities or a goal that will make you jump out of bed even before your alarm goes off, the better. The sooner you can develop a routine that works for you. Figure out how and when you work best and try to stick to it.

Get yourself to start taking notes of where you seem to concentrate the most effectively. Are you focused the most in the morning in your room, at night in the library, after class drinking coffee? Or hanging out at house parties and designing that presentation due in your communication class the following day? Look ahead and set a schedule for yourself so that you always have a time and place to be productive. And make this a priority because to graduate you must focus on graduation.

CHAPTER 2

Overcome Stress and Challenges

For me stress was having no money to buy textbooks, having little or no money to eat, colleagues and professors having a hard time understanding me, not having close friends, not being able to work off campus or find a job, not having enough time in a day. On the other hand, my challenges were that despite all that, I still needed to go to class and do homework to keep progressing.

I know by now you are wondering how I overcame those stresses and challenges. You are probably saying to yourself right now, "*I am going through the exact same thing*," or maybe you already considered quitting and giving up. Well I am sorry to tell you this, giving up is not an option for you and the fact that you are reading this book now, it will never become an option for you.

Rather than thinking negatively, I want you to start doing the opposite, until you start seeing positive results. You cannot create opportunities and overcome obstacles when you dwell on them. In order to breakthrough, you will have to see through them. You will have to use them as an instrument to motivate and uphold you. You will have to see them as enemies and roadblocks to progress.

Now, if you can see, think, imagine, and communicate your stress and challenges this way, then your mind will start developing gateways to break through, to overcome, to conquer, and to free yourself. My approach might be different from yours, my situation might be different from yours, and the way I tackle my stress and challenges might be different. But what I know for a fact is that if you are an international student, at some point you will find yourself in this predicament. You will question yourself why, and you will ask yourself several questions.

You might be lucky enough to have a family member, close friend, or host family to help reduce some of your financial stress or challenges. As for me, I had none of that. I was on my own. People that would have helped could only give me words of encouragement. No one, but you, can ever really understand your pain.

Although, I listened and took all the advice and or support I could receive, it was not enough for me to break through. These are some of the stresses and challenges I faced in college and how I overcame all of them.

Food:
I will start with food not just because, I like food, but also because food is very important. How can you survive without it? I found myself eating tenders and fries for a whole semester. Why? Because that was the only

thing I knew how to order. That was the only thing similar to the taste of chicken I am used to. It got to a point when I got to the order station they didn't even bother to ask what I would like to order because they already knew what I always ordered.

Toward the end of my first semester I got sick and tired of chicken tenders and fries. I decided to start paying more attention when people ordered different things. Now, I am an expert at ordering, lol. I was so determined, that I made friends with this African-American guy who seemed more open to learning about my culture and about me. Unlike others who felt more superior and better than Africans, Kevin was a very approachable individual. He didn't judge a book by its cover. He was open to learning about other races, especial black races. He was so interested in knowing his history. Anyway, that is a story for another day.

I started going to the bigger cafeteria with Kevin (Van Houten) and quickly ended up working at Van Houten. I was known as the king of the dish room, ha ha. Van Houten was like one of those big and expensive restaurants you see in the movies where you can eat or order anything you want, drink anything you want, serve yourself, and have a waiter over the counter serve you with special dishes.

I was so excited when Kevin took me to this place. Then he told me we had to find a table first, drop our bags, grab a drink, and finally walk around to see what we would eat. You should have seen the big smile on my face at that point. It was like Christmas day. I was not only happy because I had a variety of food and drinks to choose from, but I was also excited because I wouldn't be eating just chicken tenders and noodles anymore!

That day, I tried almost all the food and drinks they had. But the downside was I got sick for three days. So, I couldn't go with Kevin the next three days. But Kevin always made sure he told me about the menu. That's when I realized the menu changed daily. That got me so excited to the extent I started praying for a fast recovery. I started telling my mind, I am well and better already just so I could go try the new menu. According to Kevin, their fried chicken was the best. Power of the mind - we have to keep telling our inner mind we can do it, that way our entire body and mind will automatically reprogram to what we tell it to do.

The fourth day was like my birthday - the day I got to go to that cafeteria again, the day I got to try new food and their "bum ass" chicken, ha ha. This time, I dressed up nicely, like Kevin, although my pants were not all the way down like his. But I had a hat on and I was looking like, and blended in like, a typical black man in America.

At that point, I already knew the procedure. So, my focus was to eat more food, ask questions, and make more friends because I figured that was the only way I could learn more and eat more, lol. I ate a lot that day and for the first time, I fell asleep during a class lecture. I also made new friends that day. I learned that you can also place orders when the cafeteria was closed, and have your food delivered to your dorm. WOW, o yea! I couldn't wait to order, but I had no more flex-meal and I was too broke to pay cash.

By the beginning of my second semester, I was an expert in ordering anything I wanted. I was picking what to eat, where to eat, and I knew how to place delivery orders like an expert. I also had 3 side jobs I was doing to save up for my tuition and some other basic needs.

Every international student will have these challenges and eventually stress about them or even get sick like me. But what you need to do is have full control of your mind, don't be scared to try new things, don't be scared to make friends, don't be scared to be mocked and laughed at, remember your goal is not to please anyone but to making sure your health and wellbeing are taken care of.

Culture:
Before even leaving my country, my friends and family referred to me as, "America Boy" because I was already practicing and speaking like Americans. I started watching a lot of America movies. I started reading books about the culture. I started making friends on social media who lived in the states. By fall 2007, 90% of my social media friends lived in America (If you are not a member at Itoto House yet, this is a good time to join: www.itoto.org/register).

I still had to prepare my mind for the culture shock. I knew from the get go that things would be different. I knew it would be much different from home. I knew I would have to adjust. But what I didn't know is how long it would take. Just so you know, it will be different for each and every one of you, based on your interest and or concerns. But you have to start to adjust as early as possible as there are other important things you need to dedicate your mind and focus your attention on.

When I arrived, it was too different from what I had anticipated. The majority of people were nice, smiled a lot, opened and held doors open for others. It was funny to me when I got this weird and angry look from some stranger because I didn't hold the door for him. At that point I didn't know you have to hold the door behind you when someone else is behind you. Despite all this, I thought everything was genuine but later on realized just because everyone smiles all the time doesn't mean they are always happy. Just because they ask you how you are doing today doesn't mean they really care, just because they hold and open the door for you doesn't mean they think you are special or an African Prince, lol. It's just a courtesy, so get used to that and try to do it in return, so it becomes a habit. Otherwise, you could experience issues because some people are crazy. You can get beat up especially if you don't open or hold doors. I am serious. One of my friends got spat on by a crazy old lady for not holding the door for her. On the other hand, it's nice to do simple things like this. It makes others feel appreciated and loved which makes the world a happier place.

I was shocked one summer when I saw an almost naked young girl. I thought that was just something you see in the movies. But there are people who go to such an extreme. At first, I thought, either she was selling her body, or she was just crazy. Until I realized the reason was because it was summer and because it was cute. Well up till today that's not my definition of cute - sorry! Although I got used to seeing a lot of half-naked women, so it no longer bothers me. As for the men, all you need to do is just control your eyes and mind and focus on more important things. Better still, ask one out politely and they might become your girlfriend. Which leads me to my next experience: how to approach others.

When I decided to get out of my comfort zone to learn, make friends, and grow, I knew I would have to talk to people - especially to some that didn't know me. I would have to strike up a conversation. Let's start with my class experience. Most Professors want you to look directly into their eyes when talking to them. But in my culture, you are not allowed to keep direct eye contact with your superiors, especially your parents. But in the USA, it is considered inappropriate to not maintain eye contact, as you are accused of not caring or not paying attention. While in other countries, it's a sign of respect to not have direct eye contact.

It was also a challenge for me to make friends because the majority of people can hardly understand my accent and I can hardly understand people that speak really fast. So, I challenged myself to get my first girlfriend. I have always wanted to date a white girl just to verify if they are so loving, sweet, kind, and do things I was not used to, like taking someone out for dinner and paying, lol.

Well, the first girl I approached didn't want to have anything to do with me, until my Junior year. The reason why is that she was mad and angry at me for calling her fat. I didn't know it was, or could been seen, as an insult. But to me it was a great compliment. Because say a guy has a "fat" body, breast, and booty – well that would be a compliment and she had all these features. Plus, her smile was unavoidable, her hair was the greatest and most beautiful I had ever seen. But I could not even get a chance for a date because I said she was fat and I loved her, and I could see myself marrying her.

Of course, she got really scared because she thought I was weird and crazy. But to cut a long story, short it would be helpful to approach a significant other in the USA by getting to understand them and learning more about them first. Also keep in mind there are several ways to express and explain yourself when it comes to cultural differences.

The environment was also a challenge for me. During the winter it gets cold, boring, and there's hardly any outdoor activities. At that point, I was still trying to adjust. Minding the fact that, Edinboro University is in

PA, an area known for major snow storms – producing on average 6 feet of snow. And sometimes it could get colder than 30 degrees below zero!

Financial:

Every international student has his or her own imagination and conclusion about the financial aspects of any country they are going to visit for studies. Especially the United States. I believe it's the best place to be financially. Even today, I have friends who tend to want to come study or work here because they think they will automatically get richer or live more comfortably. But the truth is if you don't have a strategic plan it's not guaranteed. If you don't plan and pay attention it not going to be what you thought it would be.

There is a common saying that money doesn't grow on trees. That's 100% correct. Money comes and goes but it sure doesn't grow on trees. Before I could adjust or change my thinking and beliefs, it was too late and to this day I am still paying for debt, as a result of not properly planning. In life, most things we take for granted are the things that will hurt us the most. It is important to plan financially, especially when you have no friends, family, or support which most of us international students won't have, once we get to our chosen destination. And add to the fact that as an international student you cannot even work off campus. Getting approved to work on campus is also complicated. You will have to go through a long and complicated process to get a social security number. If and when you do, you are only allowed to work certain hours.

For the purpose of this guide book I am not going to talk about this, but I will be sure to address it later at Itoto House or in an upcoming book. What I want you to know and learn from this is to spend the little you have wisely and if you have nothing, be hungry to learn and know how to have something while focusing on your education and focusing on accomplishing your dreams. As for me I always want to look good even if I have nothing. Why? Because it makes me happy regardless of my negative situation. But sometimes what you love doing can cost you what you can't afford. There have been times my account was closed because it was overdrawn for too long. There were times, I went to a store to get something I needed so badly, knowing I didn't have the money, but still prayed and hoped my card would go through and when it didn't I walked out of the store sad, embarrassed, and frustrated.

I want you to know it will be hard for you to catch up with other people, it will be hard for you to get everything you need, it will be hard to show who you really are when many odds are against you. Even the system isn't built for you to succeed in any aspect. And even with your education, you are expected to have everything you need financially to survive all throughout your four or five years of studying. Let me tell you this, as an international student it is very important to mitigate risk. Do everything it takes to start working on your financial freedom. It's never too early to get control.

If I had control of my life 11 years ago I would be carrying shoulders like some of the richest people in the world today even though I was an international student, even though I did not have the support like they do, even though, the system did not work for me like it worked for them, even though my parents never had any savings or investments for me, even though I could not go to school for free. But what makes us different is our determination and drive. It takes a lot of courage to pack your bags and go to another country to be alone and chase your dreams. Not everyone has that courage and determination.

The things in this book are what I wish I had known when I was in your position. I can't express or explain everything I went through, but God wanted me to go through all that, so I could learn and have the required experience today to help you and many other people globally. At the end of this chapter I want you to write down your dreams, your business ideas, your positive imagination, things you love and want to do, and the kind of people and friends you want to surround yourself with. Also write down everything you think about in terms of your finances. That is the first step to making things happen. After that you need to start acting and working towards those things and when you need resources, motivation, and assistance in following through, Itoto House and our affiliates will be here to see you through.

You will be lonely, that's for sure. You will miss a lot of the things that made you feel the comforts of home. But when you are lonely, I encourage you to think, I encourage you to challenge yourself, and I encourage you to set attainable goals. I encourage you to focus on your growth rather than waiting or depending on people, social media, and society to help you. You have the bigger hand in helping yourself - no one else does.

Racism:
This is a topic I tend not to visit or speak about often. But it's very important in today's society that we speak our mind, especially when educating people on this subject. I never knew what racism meant until my second year in college. I started hearing about it from friends, in my classes, and through research. The first time I witnessed it, it affected me physically, psychologically, and emotionally. As you already know, international students are very open to trying new things and meeting people from different races but sometimes we lack networking skills - which we can help provide at www.itoto.org.

There is this very small city called Waterford located 10 to 15 miles from my school, Edinboro University. I had a friend in that city - a very nice and outgoing Caucasian woman. The city was known as "Racism City," so many African Americans don't go there. I was on my way from the club with friends, when my friend Karissa called and said she wanted to hang out with me and my friends. I told her I would drop off my friends and then come get her. While rushing to pick her up, I drove on those narrow and curvy roads that were called the backroads and very dangerous to drive through at night. As I approached a curve, a big deer came out of nowhere, so I swerved and hit some chuck of snow and crashed at the front of this dark little house that looked like a trailer.

As I was looking out of the back windshield, I saw an angry looking man with a rifle ordering me to sit on the ground or he would blow my "*Nigger*" head off. I thought he was joking. I was like, "*Sir could you help me call the cops my phone is somewhere inside the car?*" He replied and said he had already called the cops and I had to sit on the ground until they arrived. I was like, "*you've got to be kidding me. I have blood on my shirt. I just had my car totaled. I am thanking God I am alive and all you can say is sit my black ass on the snow in this cold weather?"* He then cocked his rifle.

I told myself, this man could kill me here and nobody would know and even if the cops came they could cover it up and he would get away with it. Therefore, to save my life, I did as he instructed and sat on the ground. The cops came which was another unexpected scene. Always stay calm no matter the situation you find yourself in. Don't be in a rush to speak and don't let your anger control you.

Law:
The police arrived and usually they take statements from all parties but the first thing they did was handcuff me. Then they took the man that made me sit on a cold ground with blood on me for almost an hour to a corner to take his statement. At that point, anyone could see I needed some medical attention and I was cold. So, he asked if I wanted to go to the hospital as the ambulance was on the way. I said no, I just wanted to pee and go home. He kept asking if I was the only one driving and so many other irrelevant questions. I decided to answer politely despite deep inside being so mad that I could slap the living breath out of him and his partner's mouth.

They then offered to walk me toward the bush across the street. They refused to let me urinate right there as it was against the law. He told me he was pointing the taser and would watch if I tried anything or ran, he would pull the trigger. (In my mind I was like big dumb fool where will I run to when I don't even know where I am, in pain, cold with blood on me)? I refused to go to the hospital that night as I didn't have insurance or have any other means to pay for it. They took me home that day. And while sitting in the back without handcuffs. I decided to start a conversation.

First, they changed their mood when they finally realized I was just a black man who crashed and needed help getting back to school. They started making funny jokes as to why I was going to Waterford that late and they mentioned Karissa better be very hot with some nice ass. I was like damn right, she is super-hot. They went on asking if I hit it. I was like what? Then I quickly figured out what they meant. I said no - but in the process. If you want to know the rest of the story, become a member at Itoto House and request the full story. To cut a long story short I got dropped off and still partied that night with Karissa. Her Mom ended up dropping her off when she told her the situation.

I was able to avoid police and breaking the law during my undergraduate days. After this incident, there was one more before I left school. This was after I got into a big drunken fight with another international student from Germany. He claimed he knew the law better than me and because he was white the law would work for him and against me. But little did he know I started learning and reading more about it. He charged at me on that night at one of the house parties I hosted.

By the way, I used to host parties as the VP of International Students. I was a little famous on campus, so I started a business, lol. House parties, along with a couple of other businesses I was doing.

I decided to stop running, went to the station gave my statement and my witness information. After a month of investigation, the case was dropped. Know when to teach your opponent a lesson. Don't let other people bully you because you are a minority, international student, or because they think you don't know anything or can't help yourself. Don't be scared to face your challenges because if you don't they can bring you down and add to your stress.

The last incident I had with the law was in 2014, after graduation. That is also the year I will never forget because that's the year I lost my dad. I moved to Washington State in pursuit of greener pastures after graduating in May of 2014. All my seven years in the states, I had never been handcuffed (except for when I was in Waterford). I know lots of things based on common sense. But there are other minor things I wished I had known or at least the international student's office would have lectured us on. That is local and state law. Just something general would have helped. For example, I know drunk driving is bad and risky, but I didn't know having an open bottle in your car in a parking lot was the same as drunk driving.

I almost lost my life to a cop that night trying to defend myself. But the cops were determined to take me to jail or kill me if need be. That was also one of the years cops were known for killing people of my color but at the same time they tended to always do their job. What they are not trained to do is to understand nature or medication. People react differently to medication and drugs. That night a lot went through my head and I decided to give in and let them do all they wanted as long as they didn't shoot me to death.

Afterwards, I decided to get a lawyer because I knew I wasn't guilty, not because I could afford one, but because I couldn't defend myself against the (State). I am still dealing with the court system. Why because I lost the case in 2016 after several courts, time wasted, money wasted, I couldn't afford my lawyer anymore plus it seems he was not doing his job right. I went broke paying him to not even argue with the judge. I was assigned a public defender, went to trial and lost the case. There was only one black person on the jury. Most of them were old Caucasian folks. Most of them had lost friends or a family member to drunk driving.

I did everything the court wanted me to do. They suspended my license, had me attend AA classes and treatment. I didn't need it, but the system recommended it regardless.

This is when I started studying and paying attention to the laws. The system works for those they choose it to work for. I will be blogging about this at www.itoto.org. I can't emphasize how important is it for you to register and participate because by growing together we shall be able to change the world, we shall show good examples, we shall help others grow, and we shall help save the less privileged people locally and internationally. I want you to know these few facts:

- ❖ There are always going to be a group of people that won't like you regardless of the good you do or who you are.
- ❖ No system is perfect. Even the United States system needs some work. The same for other developing countries.
- ❖ There is always going to be racism.

- ❖ There are always going to be evil people.
- ❖ There are always going to be misunderstandings and unfair judgements.

What matters is that you stay focused regardless of the stress or challenges you go through. Even if you don't understand the law or agree with certain parts of it - OBEY IT! This is especially as an international student. Remember, sorrows may last for the night, but joy comes in the morning. Good things they say don't come easily. I was down, fighting for survival, with sleepless nights. I was homeless, I slept in my car for almost an entire year. There were times I couldn't afford anything. I had to rely on friends and strangers to eat. But all those moments were to prepare me for today and tomorrow.

It's very important you do everything possible. Do everything it takes for you to survive. Being alive these days, you have to be extremely careful. You must always be alert and use common sense. We international students are more vulnerable to becoming victims. But as you read this book and practice these tips you will become the opposite of what they thought or imagine you are. You will become itoto (powerful and strong).

It's never too early to discover your passions and talents and then start putting them in action. If I had read a book like this during my college years, there are many mistakes I would not have made. There are many places I would not have gone to. There are many things I overlooked, I wouldn't have. I don't want anyone to ever make mistakes that I made in life.

Everyone in God's sight is meant to be great, but there are circumstances and situations in this life that can be major barriers. Look at the homeless today, take a look at people in jail for one reason or another, take a look at segregation, war, misunderstandings, hatred, betrayal, and many more things going on in the world today. Do you think it's all meant to be? NO! It is not. It's a fact that there are barriers. It's a fact no one is perfect. It's a fact no system is perfect. It's a fact no race is perfect. It's a fact no country is perfect. It's a fact we can be deceived easily in our society today. It's a fact greed is grown in our community, society, country, and the entire world. But I have a vision that if we, as students, can set examples, even our parents and leaders will follow and eventually the world will adjust, and the result could be that everything will become agape and amicable.

> *"There are thousands of causes for stress*
> *and one antidote to stress is self-expression.*
> *That's what happens to me every day.*
> *My thoughts get off my chest,*
> *down my sleeves, and onto my pad."*
> - Garson Kanin.

Finally, Eat, Drink, and Sleep:
Everyone already knows this, and they probably think they don't need to be reminded to do this; after all, you must eat, drink, and sleep to live and function daily. However, college life is very different. Everyone's schedules are different, from classes, side jobs, projects, sports, and recreation activities - not everyone does these things properly or similarly. Staying hydrated is good for your overall health and getting the rest you need is vital. But that doesn't mean you need to drink from the well or sleep all day.

As a college student, if you sleep too much, what will you do when you start getting old, raising a family, and building your business or career path? In college, if I get five hours of sleep I always think or feel there's something I didn't do, or something is wrong. If I was sick or drank too much, I couldn't hear my alarm go off, lol. Personally, I would say a maximum of 5 hours of sleep is enough for you. You can sleep more during the break or after graduation.

On the other hand, it is good to rest your body it will help increase your concentration the following day and freshen you mind and body. You just need to know when to go to bed and when to get out of bed. This will depend on your overall schedule. The same goes for eating well. If your throat feels parched or your stomach starts growling at you, your focus is bound to suffer. Have a small, healthy snack before getting to work, class, or practice, etc. Keep water on hand. And never forget about the importance of sleep! But, not too much sleep!

Most college students know the feeling of being in class the morning after a late night. I am guilty of this too. Sometimes, I left a party and went straight to class or work. Those days were not my best days. But I made sure I never missed work or class because if I did, I wouldn't be able to pay my bills and I wouldn't have time to catch up on assignments I was already behind on. Not getting sufficient sleep is a sure way to make you feel spacey and unmotivated. Here is a helpful resource: https://www.hindawi.com/journals/edri/2015/202753/.

Notes

Here is where you can make some notes about your dreams, your business ideas, your positive imagination, things you love and want to do, and the kind of people and friends you want to surround yourself with. Also, write down everything you think about in terms of your finances. That is the first step to making things happen.

CHAPTER 3

Communicate Your Feelings

My close friends and family usually refer to me as the quiet one. But the truth is, that is what I show them. But I can be the loudest one. Although, I like to keep my thoughts to myself. I like to pay more attention rather than be the attention. In the past year, I have come to realize it is valuable to communicate my feelings regardless of others' opinions. In fact, people will always have their own opinion which doesn't mean they are always right.

In today's society, everyone has his or her own opinion and views on different things. Everyone is allowed to speak their minds, unless you are in one of those villages in Africa where the leaders will do anything to shut you up especially when you have a forward-thinking point. Does it mean they are just so afraid of change that might make the village grow and better the lives of its citizens? Anyway, I will address that at a later stage.

Let me ask you this, has there been moment when you didn't say or communicate something just because you didn't want to be judged or perceived like someone else, then eventually something bad happened. Then you got angry at yourself for not saying something or fixing the problem. I am guilty of this and many of these situations have caused me a lot. Sometimes I get very frustrated and angry at myself and it either affects my health and or I get into trouble.

It was after the death of my dad, I decided I would not hold off anymore. I decided I would always communicate my feelings regardless of others' opinions. Since then the always feeling guilty and angry with myself part was dead. I don't tend to regret things I don't have control over anymore. Sometimes we blame nature, ourselves, and/or people around us. But I want you to know you have control of things that are happening around you, things that will happen to you, and things that you will do unto others. Before deciding if you should hold back on communicating your feelings first, ask yourself what the outcome would be, ask yourself how you will feel afterwards. If your answers are positive and uphold the greater good, then come up with a polite, and unbiased way to say whatever it is that you need to say. On the other hand, they say never rush to speak so take your time before you speak, if you need more days ask, if you need to write it down please do. What is important here is that you make sure you do not hold back, make sure you communicate your feelings and please do not wait too long.

My first year in college I regretted not telling a good friend of mine her eating habits were bad. I was like a mentor to her. I feel that if I had told her, she would not have ended up the way she is today. She would have probably never been my friend or believed in me anymore. But if I had told her and helped her by motivating her to come to the gym with me, maybe she wouldn't have end up with the body weight she has added today.

If I had communicated my feelings to a mentee of mine, he wouldn't be half paralyzed in Kenya today. But I let go because of what he would have said and because I didn't want him to see me differently as a result from giving him advice.

Don't be scared to lose friends. Don't be scared if people walk out on you. Don't be scared if people judge you differently. Sometimes it is better to lose friends, have people walking out on you, and people will always judge you regardless. So therefore, do yourself a favor and always communicate your feelings regardless of other people's opinions.

For years, I was mad at the women that I had always and will always love unconditionally. I was frustrated that she was never there for me even when I started becoming a man. I tried to understand why the woman that brought me into this world and believed in me, always telling great things about me, always encouraging me, always empowering me, always interceding for me, but once when I needed her to understand why I am not perfect and why I made a useless mistake, she couldn't. I personally couldn't understand that. Until I put myself in her shoes which was very difficult because I am not a woman or built to feel the things women do or act like one but as soon I got into the psychological thinking of that and the fact I already know nobody is perfect, it opened up my eyes.

Just the way this book is already getting you thinking about important things you never thought about, that is the same feeling I have had in several instances. There is a saying, *only he who wears a shoe truly knows how it hurts*. On the other hand, it's hard for others whether blood or not, to understand where you hurt. Even me writing this, do not. I can only imagine. So, I advise you today, speak your mind regardless of other's opinions. Yes, they might hate you for that, but believe me you'll feel better and relieved when you do. After you speak your mind all you have to do is watch. Just keep telling yourself at least now, they know. So, watch and see whatever they come up with or do with it. Remember it won't always be the results you are expecting but don't be disappointed just like you already know you don't have control over the weather that's how you won't have control over others.

I want you to know today as a student you won't always have control over your job, people, society, friends, family, or the law. But what you do have control over are your words, actions, dedication, commitment, decisions, approach, and execution. Nobody will force you to commit suicide, nobody will force you to put your hand in a fire, unless they want to kill you and make you suffer and if that point is clear, all you can do is fight.

I have had to fight all my life. I will keep fighting because when you are unique and blessed, the world and people will talk about you. They will try to stop you. They will try to bring you down. Make a difference, set standards, be a great example. When people start telling you "Oh you think you're better," of course you're better if anyone can say that to your face it's clear you're better because you never say you're better that's one way for people to put you down.

And remember never think you're better. All fingers are not equal. All you have to do is make people around you and people you believe in bring the best in them and set boundaries because you can only try as they have control over their actions just like you do. Before I figured out so many things I just wanted to talk a lot, I mean a lot, a whole lot. Just like a police officer will tell you, you have the right to remain silent for anything you say can be used against you in the Court of Law. Please students, understand that there are times when you should not speak. When I say communicate your feelings regardless of others' opinions, I don't mean you should put yourself at risk.

> *"Being in control of your life and having*
> *realistic expectations about your day-to-day challenges*
> *are the keys to stress management,*
> *which is perhaps the most important ingredient to*
> *living a happy, health,y and rewarding life."*
> - Marilu Henner

Finally, Set Goals and Follow Through
To stay focused in life we need to set goals and follow through with them. We also need to consistently make adjustments and reevaluate those goals

in order to be competitive, get good grades, be the best in everything you do you. You must be also be flexible with your daily, weekly, monthly, and yearly schedule. I never knew the importance of this, when I was in college. So, doing these things at my first job after college was very challenging.

Sometimes, I get so disorganized that it affects my work performance. Not only will setting goals and following through help you graduate on time, but also it will prepare you for your professional career and future. You will be able to fit in perfectly even better than people who never knew this from the get go. You have to be really sure of what it is that you want to get done, how you want it done, and when you want it done.

Every semester is different, and every year will be different, so learn to set goals and follow through with them while mastering the ability to adjust and evaluate so you don't get burned out or miss out on things that are outside your goals. If you have homework in several classes, various ongoing projects already assigned, and tests to study for, you're likely to stay more overwhelmed than focused. This is why it's important to set goals. What is the most important thing you need to do right now? You can only really focus on one thing at a time, so decide on some realistic goals before setting out a game plan to tackle those goals.

Notes

What are your top goals? Do you have a plan to achieve your goals? Are there any communications challenges that you face right now?

CHAPTER 4

Understand Your Strengths and Weaknesses

This is a very important tip especially if you are focusing on results and success. One of the fundamentals to getting positive results and becoming successful is to understand your strengths and weaknesses. If you can understand these two important things and know when to utilize each and when to stop, you will find yourself winning even when others don't see it that way.

I know who I am. I already knew this *before* I left Africa, on a scholarship, after acing my TOEFL and SAT exams. While others were complaining about studying and preparing to take the necessary tests, I was busy studying and practicing. I was busy researching and I was busy learning how to become successful in surviving educationally in a foreign country. But little did I know, I had to study the media too.

My strength was my ability to focus regardless of what I saw, what I heard, what people said, what the media said, and what everybody else said. All my focus was on my commitment to study hard and pass my tests, so I could apply to several schools and get scholarships. My strength was knowing I would be successful, knowing I would stand out, knowing I would make it and knowing I would become who my inner-mind told me I would. This is regardless of anyone else's opinion including my friends, family, and the world.

There was a time when I did not watch my mouth and talked back to an officer in a uniform and told him, "*I make more money than you and don't hate that my car is better than yours because I worked hard for it, so, please go do your job.*" I did not know I pissed him off. He was bothering me in a parking lot. So, he had to use everything he learned at the police academy to take me in and put me in the books and system and being a minority made it extremely worse. Until this day, I still pay for that mistake.

So, as an international student who is not indigene, please keep quiet when indigenous law officers try to talk to you because they know the law better and for the fact we aren't from here and the law was not part of our SAT and TOEFL. We need to respect and accept their power because our own well-being is at stake. Still, to this day, I keep this belief.

I once dated a beautiful, lovely and loyal lady who brought me to Seattle, WA. We attended Gannon University together, but she works for the government now and I believe she is a top-secret agent. I never wanted to go to Seattle. My dream was to be in L.A. because I have always wanted to go and build an empire there. Why? Because that is the most diverse city in the United States. But, the power of a woman and being in love convinced me to realign.

Even when I drove a thousand miles to move her there, we almost crashed before Montana. But I was able to save our lives and it was a miracle. She couldn't thank me enough and I couldn't thank the Lord enough. But life made us part ways when her fellow law officials tried to threaten me like every other black person they had encountered. Little did they know, people are different regardless of color. I knew how she disliked the Job despite the fact she studied biology in college, but her title and pay were legit at that time.

Anyway, that is what I am trying to say here. What I want you as an international student to know is your strength whether you or anyone agreed to it or not you have to know and understand it, to become who you are really meant to be. It takes special people to understand a lot of things and to act the way they need to act. It took me too long to know this. I made a lot of mistakes and I don't want you to make similar mistakes. I don't want you to get carried away like I was. I don't want you to pay the price I paid when you really don't have to. I don't want you to get tied up with the legal system like I was but what I want you to do is understand your strength, inner power, and mental capacity. Others don't need to understand you, others don't need to agree with you, others don't need to follow you. UNDERSTAND YOUR STRENGTH.

Everyone has a unique power and understanding. Everyone knows what they want as long as it's positive and it is in the universal aspect of life. Even the heavens will see you through and your beliefs will make you stand out even in the midst of your obstacles. Identify your strength my fellow student, your location is just a location your current situation is just a situation. Your studying is to better you, your studying is to make you stand out. Therefore, identifying your strength is vital and crucial. It is the core to your survival and breakthrough. "Only the strong survive they say" so shall you when you discover your strength.

If you have ever seen the movies/shows Troy, Vikings, Game of Thrones etc. and many others, you will know your strength can take you places. When I validated my strength I became immeasurable, I became unimaginable, I became greater, I became unstoppable, I became unspeakable, and I became FOCUS. I Focused like I have never done before. I became more supportive, I became more like a changemaker. Even the fact that I don't care about my public image or likes, or what-so-evers, shows my strength.

As a result, I became an impact, I became change, I became a better mentor, I became a better investor, I became a better programmer, I became a better scientist, I became a better discoverer, I became a better solicitor, I became more powerful, I became unimaginable just to name a few. I want you to become powerful too.

> *"When I'm grateful for all the blessings,*
> *it puts away all the stress about things not in my control. Things like long*
> *hours, aging, pollution, scandals ... it helps me create perspective by just*
> *focusing on being grateful. Take that moment twice a day with yourself."*
> - Darby Stanchfield

Finally, Limit Your Social Media Consumption

Facebook! Facebook!, Facebook!, Facebook!, Facebook!, Snapchat!, Snapchat!, Snapchat!, Snapchat!, Snapchat!. Ask yourself a few questions and I want you to answer yourself honestly. How much have you made from Facebook, Snapchat, Instagram, or Twitter? How many school projects have you completed that required you to spend hours, days, weeks, months, the time you currently spend on those platforms? If you have made money or complete a graded school project with social media, I want to hear from you because I have $500 for you just to hear your story and see your proof of how you made money or completed the project with social media.

As a matter of fact, many of us are guilty when it comes to wasting time on these platforms. I believe 7 out of 10 of you at some point you have wished you never spent the amount of time you spent on social media because you finally realized you could have gotten a lot of homework done during that lost time. You could have been making money or you could have caught up on sleep.

We all know time is valuable and time is money. I was guilty of this and I always wished if I had known better the amount of time I spent on social media in college, if I had spent that same amount of time working on my dreams, I would have been at least 20% richer and 35% more productive at what I spend my valuable time doing today. We need to realize all these platforms are not going anywhere. There are many more to come. There was no Snapchat during my college days and all these platforms were not that intriguing and were less valued. As a college student from an international background, instead of spending so much time on Facebook, pick up a new hobby, pick up a book, or better still join us at Itoto House and be a helpful resource for another student.

Information is the key - we don't know what we don't know. If we can share our experiences with our fellow students, we will not only help them grow, but we are working to make ourselves better in order to help each other succeed in our different callings. Depending on your internet habits, this one can be a little tough to follow at first. For many college students, checking social media favorites like Facebook and Twitter has become a reflexive habit. Just keep reminding yourself that you don't need to check these sites every time you use your computer for school or work or pick up your phone. Make sure you logout and focus on the tasks at hand. This is very important.

Facebook and any other platform will still succeed and make profit even if you don't check your profile, post, or comment on other profiles. But on the other hand, you can lose money, turn in a project late, get fired from your job, or even miss class by utilizing those platforms more than you should. It may seem harmless to go through your networks quickly just to get the feeling of obligation out of the way, but it's easy to get sucked into a time warp this way. If you know that you're someone who easily loses track of time on social networks, or if you always end up going back to them every ten minutes, then consciously limit yourself. Facebook just isn't conducive to getting work done, as much as we all wish it were.

Notes

What are your weaknesses? How can you improve in those areas? What are your strengths? How can your strengths help you to achieve your goals?

CHAPTER 5

Study Your Environment, Your People, and Your World

We all know the saying, *"save the best for last."* I think I just did. I want you to take a few minutes and think about every successful person you know. Think about your role models, think about your favorite artists, public figures, or someone famous who is your role model. Right down that person's name and the top ten reasons why they are your role model. When you are done I also want you to write down why you think they are famous, rich, and well known and why they inspire you. What do you think makes them special or unique, compared to others?

Why am I asking you to do this exercise? Because it will help you understand the vision exercise you will participate in, at the end of this chapter. It will help you study and know your dreams, your family, and your approach to respond. If you can control the way you respond to these things everything else is nothing major because these things are the most influential attributes to your success.

Let me tell you this - everyone wants to be successful but not everyone is successful. Why? Take a few minutes to think about it. Stop reading until you have answered this question. Write your thoughts here. What do you think makes a person successful?

This section is meant to be interactive to help you discover your inner most desires and wants so you can easily separate them from just mere needs.

Before I took the SAT and TOEFL tests, all I wanted was to do all it took to get the best education. My parents wanted that for me, but they could not afford it. Yet they tried so hard to convince me not to travel - especially my dad. I later learned why he didn't wanted me to go to the United States. It was not because he was once an international student in the states too but because his experience wasn't very positive, and this was way back when things were more at ease in terms of jobs and finances, before the government started stricter laws.

To cut a long story short, I traveled and made it happen because it was in my hands. I know my dreams and what I can do to achieve them. I knew no one else could ever understand me the way I understand myself, not even my parents. Let me ask you this, have you ever had a conversation with your parents and they responded as if they knew what you were thinking but it turned out they were totally wrong?

If your answer is yes or close, does it make sense if I tell you that you have control and power over how you respond and react to every opinion or decision others make on your behalf? It took me 31 years about to be 32 and writing this guide book to figure out how to respond to family, people, associates, partners, and the world entirely. People will expect certain things and responses from you and when you don't give them the action or response they are looking for they will become disappointed. It is like when your teacher quizzes you but only he or she knows the answers even though there are several ways to answer the question they can deduct a point or give you no points.

I want you to think about a similar scenario, at least five where anyone could expect a particular response from you, but your response was off. Write those down. From my experience it is better to shut up and let the other person do the talking and most times they will answer themselves and all you have to do is agree completely or agree to disagree. I say study and know your dreams, family, and your approach to respond to situations. This sets you up for success. Your words can hurt, kill, bless and/or sustain, so making good use of them is very important. Knowing when to agree or disagree is very important. There are many other things I will help you accomplish as you continue to work with my team and me.

There are several resources out there that most international students will not be aware of. This could be important information that non-international students or other people know, but you don't. On the other hand, nobody knows it all. What I can tell you is that you know it all on how to control your response to a situation. You know how to get answers to specific questions.

As a sales representative and a business development executive I have been through a lot of training locally and internationally. I have worked for top 100 companies just to name a couple Microsoft, Verizon wireless, etc. But my favorite sales training was Questions Based Selling QBS. Thomas Freeze is one of my mentors. I met him a few times and he personally signed some of his books I have read. One thing I can say that has boosted my success in a sales career is QBS, that's why I still use it today. QBS can help you uncover a lot of information by giving others the opportunity to speak and explain their concerns, pain points, needs, desires, and wants.

Folks, as an international student, please stop doing the talking rather doing the listening. It will be more beneficial for you to listen than to talk. Only talk when you need to communicate - speak your mind, ask questions, give an opinion, make a sales pitch, etc. Like the cops say, "*you have the right to remain silent because anything you say can be used against you in the court of law.*"

We international students tend to rush into explaining ourselves all the time and the more we explain the less people can understand us, so why waste your time. They say, *actions speak louder than words.* Let our actions speak for us. Let me tell you this - your mind will become your greatest weapon - it can make or destroy you. So, the earlier you take control of your mind, the better. By now you should know there are odds against your success and some of you know why. Some of you don't know, some of you can guess, some of you don't have any clue about it.

It is very important to control your mind. How can you win the war against the world if you can't even win or control the war against your mind? We are victims of our minds. Sometimes our minds tell us to do things that are detrimental to our success. The mind can make us do things and we will regret the outcome afterwards, when it's too late. Many mistakes we make in life are the result of what we process in our minds, influenced by what our parents say or think about us, what our family members say and think about us, what other people and friends think about us, what the world thinks about us.

You can never win if you keep living in that mindset. You will be giving the world another reason to see you as a loser or loner. Even your family will sometimes disagree with you, not because they don't care or don't love you, but because they have certain expectations for you. They naturally want you to do certain things and act in a certain way. When you start asking specific questions you will start understanding a lot of things and the various scenarios will start to make sense. Words are just words until they have been acted on by you.

Start asking your family, friends, professors, and yourself specific questions. For example, *Please, help me understand. How do you mean? Can you please clarify? If I understand you correctly, you mean_____? How do you want me to accomplish this? What do you need from me? What do you want from me?*

Needs and wants can be mistakenly used in the same context. But these are two different things.

Study body language and pay attention to what others are communicating. This will help you clarify and understand people better. There are good people out there but paying attention to what is going on in society today, it is clear that there are many bad people as well. Many people are even killing each other.

While I was writing this book, watching TV on a beautiful Saturday morning, I saw on CNN that a young black college kid from Michigan shot and killed his parents. The first thing that came to my mind was that there is no good reason in the world that would make someone kill their parents. Then I started thinking to myself there must have been a disconnect at some point. Parents not understanding their kid and the kid not understanding his parents. Law officers revealed that prior to interviewing the boy, he didn't make any sense as if he was on drugs. This is where they could have asked specific and detailed questions and paid attention to specific answers and details.

High Schools and colleges are targets these days for bad people who want to cause harm. Have you asked yourself why? Why can't they go after the law, government, and big corporations? Why even make such decisions? Well this all has something to do with the mind. It is important to have control over your mind, understand, study, and learn about people by asking specific questions. This won't just make you understand the world better, but it will have you better yourself, it will help you control your actions, it will help you pinpoint upcoming bad or evil situations.

So many innocent students have lost, their life, because of psychopaths, because of people who cannot control their mind and emotions. Why do we have to pay for other people's mistakes? Why do people have to suffer because of the misguided decisions of others. If schools are targeted these days, then I tell you it's time to equip yourself. It's time to engage, educate, encourage, and empower yourself.

We can help you with this and provide
many additional benefits
through Itoto house organization.

The more information we have the more educated we are the powerful we become. Although our lives are still not 100% guaranteed, we can take control of our minds. We can then respond to things around us carefully and positively. If we are not the target for the bad and evil people, we can now be the solution and an example to change the world.

Learning in today's society is very powerful compared to the ways our forefathers learned. The power of IOT is becoming more scientific and it can be good or bad. I have seen a lot of bad about it these days but the only people benefiting are the big corporations, government, media and law enforcement just to name a few. How can we students benefit, rather than being a target? Always ask questions and seek knowledge that will be the subject of my next book.

Like I promised in this book, I will do all it takes to make every student successful. If I had known the things I know today, 10 years ago, I wouldn't have made all the bad decisions I made in the past. I would be 10x better than what I am today. Maybe I would be the next Mark Zuckerberg! But unfortunately, I am not. I found my joy, my blessing and my dream and if I become the next Mark while chasing my dreams to bring global positive change in the world, so be it. I know you reading this book have a great mind. Not because you are a student but because of the fact that you are even taking time out to read this book right now. It means you care about yourself. It means you want to be great. It means you want to help change the world. It means you have the great desire to be a changing force, and we will together accomplish this change, so we can set great examples for the bad and evil people out there.

Most times it's better to shut up than speak, most times it's better to ask questions than answer questions. Always ask specific and clarifying questions, especially when you can hardly understand the accent of others, it makes it difficult to understand. So, always listen carefully and pay attention in class, outside of class, in meetings, while working on a project, at church or at mosque, at gatherings, and all around you.

Remember, never depend on anyone else to make you happy or to understand you the way you understand yourself. The truth is no one will make you happy. You alone can make yourself happy. How? By following these 5 important FOCUS steps, always seeking knowledge, asking, discovering, and asking specific questions. You will be able to understand and uncover so many things and by doing so you can more easily control the way you will react to others. It will be difficult for anyone to take your happy from you.

Although, this doesn't mean there won't be other people around you that will disagree with you, hate your drive, and look for several ways to bring you down just because they are down. All you can do is spot those types of people and learn how to interact with them if you really need to.

FOCUS to Succeed in School and in LIFE!
My hope is that you now have a clearer understanding of the 5 success actions that can fuel your success. They are:

1. **F**ocus on graduation.
2. **O**vercome stress and challenges.
3. **C**ommunicate your feelings regardless of the opinion of others.
4. **U**nderstand your strengths and weaknesses.
5. **S**tudy your environment, your people, and your world.

These 5 important factors will help you to become one of the international students who succeed in achieving the dreams you have worked so hard for. This will also be the first huge step in achieving your full potential.

Finally Reward Yourself
Do you think you deserve some credit if you follow these tips and meet your goals? You do! There's nothing like a little reward to keep your motivation up. Think little things at first. Say you need to start working on an essay—you might decide to gift yourself a tasty treat once you get the paper outlined. Don't take a bite out of that cookie until you've met

your stipulation though; you will only be cheating yourself in the end! Don't go overboard by thinking up too many rewards for yourself but do think of nice ways to give yourself a break after making good progress. If you're a social media junkie, you could even allow yourself some guilt-free social media time as a reward after getting some work done. You'll feel less overwhelmed if you have incentives to keep you going bit by bit.

Additional Tips

1. Focus on being the best and what you're good at: eventually do what you always planned to do after graduation even if you change majors.
2. Stay away from trouble. Understand the law and obey the law.
3. Have fun and be smart about it: activities, new adventures, relationship, experience the culture.
4. Don't forget where you are from and be open: always stay in touch with family and friends back home.
5. Build your credit when possible: credit is king in the USA: cash is king in developing countries.
6. Stay in your lane. Don't try to be who you are not. Don't bend to peer pressure.
7. Most importantly, KNOW THAT YOU CAN DO IT! I am here to help, and I created Itoto House to help you too.

More Tips and Inspiration from the ITOTO Blog

by Felix Eshesimua

See all of our blog posts at:
https://itoto.org/blogs

Transitioning to Adulthood
5/2/2017

Moving from under that thumb of our parents to making decisions as adults is a hard transition. One that most of us don't make gracefully. We stumble and make bad decisions. And if we are lucky we make it through without any permanent damage.

However, making this transition while attending college adds a whole other level of difficulty. It's a rite of passage that many struggles with for years before they finally get it right. And the rest of us may never reach that point. The purpose of this article is to explore some of those challenges and give advice that will hopefully help you to overcome those hurdles.

First, just because you are on your own, does not mean you won't need help. Being an adult is not doing everything by yourself, it's managing what you have and knowing when to reach out for support. If you need help with income, studying or just some other essentials, use the resources around you. Learning this lesson sooner than later will save you a lot of stress.

Second, academics are not as you are used to them being. With no one to answer to about your grades and work, it can become very easy to slack off. But remember these courses are harder so they will take more work. And as you are now paying for your education, you should allow yourself to become more motivated about school. You are responsible for your own assignments, no one is going to remind you to turn things in or study. This is also a good time to realize that you will need to attend class even when you don't want to. All very important lessons that will transfer over to your everyday life and make you a successful adult.

Third, you will be around a lot of that college life you saw on tv. The invitations to infinite parties, drinking, sex and other things are going to be thrown in your face constantly. They key is to prioritize. Handle your important tasks first. Next don't forget who you are and what you stand for. And then do everything in moderation. It may all seem like good fun at first, but you don't want to end up allowing something to monopolize your life that is not beneficial.

Third, relationships will become harder. When you are not consistently seeing friends, family and significant others, it can put a strain on your relationship. You will need to learn to balance everything, while still making time for loved ones. This is a hard task, but others will understand as life begins to get busy. It is something that may always be a struggle but will show you the true strength behind the relationship.

Everyone understands how hard this transition will be. After all, one week you have to check in with your parents for everything and the next you are a free agent. It's a hard adjustment and no one expects you to get it right immediately. Just take your time, ask for help when it's necessary, don't lose who you are in all the craziness of college life and make time for those you love. Reach out to your mentors if you need help and advice.

The Power of Focus
5/7/2017

I am focused.
Are YOU?
What have you done recently to work toward achieving your dreams?
What have you achieved in life that you are most proud of?

Let me tell you a true story about how far you can go with the Power of Focus.

Ten years ago, I had a vision. It was a vision to make this world a better place - a better place for everyone, regardless of location, gender, religion, ethnicity, sexual orientation, race, or color. As I grew older, my dreams started to become a reality.

Today, I am actively developing a digital community for international students across the globe. It's a chance for students to connect digitally and personally, and it's a chance for me to help people and continue to develop others. It's also a chance to watch my vision come to fruition.

The power of focus has exposed my inner mind as to why there are so many ungodly things going on in the world today. With the power of focus, you can have a clear idea of your dreams. You can easily get back up when you fall. You can fight your enemies spiritually.

You can clearly see whenever God wants to speak to you in the spirit realm through vision. You can begin to understand why there is so much hate, jealousy, discrimination, and gossip in this world. You can understand why the world is imperfect. The power of focus allows you to understand yourself better and what plan God has for you.

Today, I encourage every student to take a few days to focus on you. Discover yourself. Find your inner thoughts. Create a plan, have faith, and stay focused - no matter what life throws at you.

Stay tuned for more life stories of what I have achieved through being focused and how the power of focus has kept me alive.

Tips for Upcoming Graduates
5/17/17

Your graduation date is getting near. You've spent 4 years or more at a higher education institution, and most of your life preparing for the moment when you start your own rewarding career. You have studied hard. You have memorized ridiculous equations and lots of random facts you will never use. You have plenty of memories and lots of knowledge you are ready to put to work.

With everything that you know, do you feel prepared for your first real job?

Though you may answer with a ready yes, there are some things that you can still do to better prepare yourself for the future. Getting ready to look for a job in your career field, you know to begin with research into the field and maybe even read a few articles. Here are a few more steps to assist you in your search and to ensure you success in whatever you do:

First and foremost, you need to create and/or update your LinkedIn account. This will turn out to be a very important resource in not only helping you to find a job but allowing you to see information on the companies you are applying for. It also allows you to network with other professionals and even get endorsements for your skills. These are basically people saying that "Yes, they can do this, and I can vouch for them."

Secondly, internships are very vital. Apply for internships, as these are considered work experience. They allow for you to get understanding and see what it is that you will actually be doing. It is also an excellent way to prove yourself in high demand fields.

Get a mentor. This will be your most valuable asset. Mentors are meant to guide you and give you sound wisdom. They can help you walk through issues from deciding what your specialty should be in if you should move out of state/country for a job. There are people at Itoto organization who have been where you are.

Recognizing the Signs of Depression
5/29/2017

> *"Every man has his secret sorrows*
> *which the world knows not;*
> *and often times we call a man cold*
> *when he is only sad."*
> – Henry Wadsworth Longfellow

The signs of depression are not always as obvious as crying, suicidal actions or cutting. Most people who are either are really good at hiding it or do not recognize the signs in themselves. Did you know that 1 in 4 college students suffer from some form of mental illness, including depression? About 44% of college students report having signs of depression and 75% do not seek help. Young people who are diagnosed with depression are 5 time more likely to attempt suicide than adults. Suicide is the third leading cause of depression among college students. According to statistics, 19% of young people in the US will contemplate or attempt suicide every year, 4 out of 5 college students who contemplate or attempt suicide will have clear warnings signs. We need to educate ourselves to catch the warnings before they are too late. In this article we will learn to recognize depression and what to do to help.

First, recognize the signs.
Loss of interest- someone who is suffering from depression will no longer enjoy the things they once did. They may seem distant and disinterested and not want to participate in things they normally do.

Sleep difficulties- often times they will have a hard time falling or staying asleep. They may be restless and yet still exhibit signs of extreme exhaustion.

Eating habits- A person suffering from depression will either eat a lot as eating provides some sort of comfort, or they will eat very little as they are overwhelmed with their emotions.

Anger or irritability- They will be easily angered or provoked, often becoming irritated at the most simple, small things

Negative/suicidal thoughts and comments- This is an obvious one. Some people will tell you where they are and what they are feeling. These comments should never be taken lightly, and they may say it in passing or jokingly.

Loss of confidence- Another obvious sign. When a person loses the confidence in themselves, they lose the will and strength to be themselves. This is a very dangerous sign.

Recklessness- This can be defined by excessive drinking, partying and other things that are not characteristic. When someone is willing to take more risks, they are looking for either an escape, or a way to feel.

Most people who are suffering don't know how to come out and ask for help. Depression is made fun of and often ridiculed. And due to people using it as a tool to get attention, many people who are suffering go unheeded. But not that you recognize the signs, what do you do?

The second step is helping.

Listen- allow them to talk. Sometimes allowing someone to vent is the best way to help.

Don't push too hard- if they don't want to talk, do not try to force them too. You may end up pushing them away or deeper into their depression.

Encourage activity- suggest outings or things to help cheer them up. It is best not to leave someone suffering with depression alone as they will isolate themselves and make things worse. Be gentle but invite them to participate and get out of their comfort zone.

Create a stable environment- try to reduce the amount of stress in the environment and person's life. Stress can create the feeling of failure which adds to depression.

Encourage to seek and stick with treatment- do not be an enabler. This may save their lives.

Emphasize that this is not permanent- Be reassuring and let them know that this can be cured, it can be managed, and will not last forever.

Lastly, never, ever, tell someone to get over it. Emotions will affect us all differently, and we will react differently. Remember to be aware, considerate, diligent and encouraging. There are literally lives at stake.

Global Love!
Itoto Team

Saving Money in College
10/8/2017

First, buy used or rent text books. I remember standing in the bookstore with a dumfounded look on my face when the clerk told me my chemistry text book was $400.00. This did not include the lab book and other tools I needed for the class. I ended up borrowing the book from a friend who had just finished the class, but it opened my eyes to the world of used text books and borrowing. The next semester I spent 150.00 on books for all 4 classes.

Second, reduce impulse buys. I know light saber chop sticks, and a lava lamp seem like great investments. And going to see the newest marvel creation 60 times is very rewarding. However, these are huge guzzlers of money that you need. Be wise in what you pay for and always thing over your options and beyond the moment.

Third, create a food budget. Often times late night taco bell runs, and name brand foods freezer foods are how we survive. However, in a week's time you have wasted over $100 and have nothing to show for it. You can take the same $100 and go grocery shopping and have food for two weeks. Also, learn to cook. It will save you money.

Fourth, always be on the lookout for scholarships. That's less money out of your pocket. Also sell your old text books. If you no longer need it, that can be good cash in your pocket and less clutter in your room.

Fifth, open a bank account. Outside of the obvious reasons to have an account, there is one great benefit that I have personality noticed. It's harder to spend money that isn't in front of you and easily accessible.

Sixth, pay yourself. Whenever you get money always put aside some portion of it for saving. Whether it be 5 or 50, it all builds up and is great when you get into a pinch.

Seventh, this will be the hardest. It may be time to ditch cable. Netflix and Hulu will give you the same benefits but cost significantly less.

Eighth, it's ok to stay home. Know your budget and what you can afford. Live within your means. If you can't afford a night on the town, there is no shame on in that.

Ninth, learn to bargain shop. Good Wills and thrift shores will save you on everything you could need. That is a promise.

Tenth, and last, transportation. You will spend money on transportation either way. Just be smart about it. If it's a manageable bus ride, then leave your car at home. Don't be afraid to walk or ride your bike. And carpooling is an option.

These are easy and quick ways to start saving money and cutting corners. However, the real key is dedication. You have to stick with your budget no matter how many sales your favorite store puts on. Good luck!

Knowledge Is Like a Garden if it Is Not Cultivated, it Can NOT Be Harvested.
10/22/2017

But this is what surprised me every time I ask a simple question it was either my question was funny, they couldn't understand my accent, or they see the fact I am very new to the environment. But what they didn't know is that I have been here before, I have heard, and I have seen but It won't prevent me from learning as a result, I had to ask truthful and direct questions. Knowledge is something every human have regardless of color the truth is how you use it, how you want to use it, how you want to be seen using or even if you want to use it at all that is where the difference would be.

I will be short because I learn from traveling a lot, listening to educated people like myself, listening to mentors, listening to people with power, and people with wealth. One thing I learn is been brief and SILENCE IS THE KEY TO THE UNEXPECTABLE OUTCOME. I decide to put this to practice and I found out it's a truth statement even though it took me a decade to figure that out. When you ignore racism, gossip, haters, conditional approaches, stereotyping, just to name a few you become more powerful, and causing no harms to people and the entire world.

To sum this truthful and maybe complicated story up: (It's an Africa Provide and a true Africa story, meaning if you don't work every day to acquire knowledge regardless of money and power, and you don't know knowledge you have acquired and put it in place DON'T EXPECT TO GAIN ANYTHING FROM IT. Your Knowledge is USELESS without making a different. Anyone can have money and society power but not everyone can make change.

I will continuously strive to explain true fact we humans ignore that has and keep causing global trouble and war. For now, I will stay brief. Until then pay attention to all our introduction articles.

Stay tuned!
We Powerful, Educated, Healthy, and Strong!

Itoto House: New Home for International Students
By Itoto House Organization
12/10/2017

Studying in a foreign country is tough. New faces, new culture, new customs and new law can make one feel alienated abroad. But not anymore. A revolutionary student assistance program has come up to make lives simpler for international students in foreign countries. Titled as "<u>Itoto House Organization</u>", the program aims to engage, educate and empower international students with the required know-how to thrive successfully in a new country through its global community of college scholars and volunteer mentors. It's free to register with Itoto House.

How Itoto House can help you?

Itoto House is the first ever & fastest growing student assistance program specifically designed for international students across the globe, irrespective of caste, color, sexual orientation, creed and ethnicity. The primary goal of the program is to make transitions easier for international students who often have to adjust to new environments while studying abroad. From the laws & regulations to the society as a whole to the career scene to even making friends and building relationships in a foreign country- the program gears to help international students with all needed information.

What separates <u>Itoto House</u> from its similar counterparts is that it's no one-size-fits-all program. The program treats each member or student individually to ensure the best solution and advice as per his or her specific needs.

Itoto House can be defined as the 'Google' for international students. The program will provide you the needed knowledge, advice and tips about anything that you want to know about the new country where you have flown to study. We know how tough it could be to survive in a new country where everything is almost different from your homeland. We are dedicated to creating the feel of 'home away from home' even when you are miles away from your native country.

The Idea Behind Itoto House

Felix Eshesimua, founder of Itoto House himself was an international student from West Africa who migrated to the USA to study at Edinboro University, Pennsylvania. He was mesmerized by the dreamy picture of America as is shown by the African media. But as he arrived in the States, he realized it's no dreamland and one has to work really hard to make a living. He also saw how the American media depicts Africa and other countries in a negative light. Worst, he had to face lot of discrimination, segregation & invalid judgment. His experiences in America inspired him to fix the issues of media and simultaneously create a program that will help to make lives better for many international students struggling hard in foreign countries like him.

Felix started mentoring freshmen from Africa in College at Edinboro University of Pennsylvania and Gannon University and gradually his efforts snowballed into a full-fledged student assistance program. Thus, Itoto House was born it was a part of Felix's project in the final year of his college. Today, the organization is growing globally and by the end of 2018, Felix is hopeful to be able to train/hire engagement representatives to grow further and reach out to more students.

Itoto House is geared to make international students bold and powerful so that they can bring out the best in them. The best part is that you will receive mentoring from people who have walked in your shoes earlier and are able to understand your situation from your perspective. We are building a sensible, knowledgeable and empathetic community where everyone will receive equal respective, regardless of location, culture, sex or race. We welcome you to a house where everybody is a member of a huge diverse family. We are looking forward to making the world a better place to live in.

3.8 Million Mobile International Students
Predicted by 2024
12/28/2017

India and China will contribute 35% of the global growth in international students while the most popular education destinations – the USA, UK, and Australia – will continue to attract the largest numbers of students. The emerging host countries such as China and Malaysia will be much more competitive. The new major sending countries, such as Nigeria, Saudi Arabia, and Indonesia, will make their way to the top. The research includes analyses of three scenarios in international education, in order "to better understand the possible effects of the future global environment". The report is not openly available and can be purchased from the British Council for US $250.

The researchers have found out that the global gross HE ratio will continue to rise until 2024, and overall enrolments will increase by 32 million – 1.4% – a year, to 196 million worldwide. India's enrolment growth will be the highest in the world. It is predicted that by 2024, India, China, Indonesia and the USA would be home to more than half of the world's students in the age range 18-22 years. Although recent years have seen the growth of around 6% a year, the British Council research maintains that the numbers of "outbound mobile" international students in the whole world would grow by on average 1.8% a year and would reach 3.85 million by 2024.

The dominating sending countries it seems would continue to be China and India, sending huge students flows to the United States and the United Kingdom. By 2024, the mobile student population from China is forecast to be 855,000 while India will send 376,000 students – together contributing a third of all mobile students globally. Although China is rapidly developing its own HE system, and therefore the demand among Chinese students to study abroad may decline.

The report also says that Germany could become the third largest sender of students by 2024 while "Saudi Arabia, Nigeria, Nepal, Pakistan, Iraq, Brazil, Turkey, and Indonesia will emerge as important origin markets."

Such host countries as the USA, Britain, Australia, Germany, and Canada will continue to be the world's major destinations of international students, according to the British Council report. America will be the "major beneficiary" of growth in student mobility from China and India, while Britain will benefit from the large markets of India, Nigeria, Saudi Arabia and Pakistan. The research forecasts that India will replace China as the UK's top student sender.

Growth in international students going to Australia will be even slower, largely because of a strong currency and the high cost of living, with the country attracting only an extra 71,000 students by 2024, the council forecasts. In terms of host countries, the British Council report predicts that China, Malaysia and maybe India could become major host countries in the coming decade.

What Is Bothering You?
1/17/2018

I was talking to myself
A strange voice in my head
Told me to go ahead
But I paused
I asked what if I give my all?
What if there's nothing left to fight for?
What if all my labor yields no result?
What if I thought it will work and it didn't work?
What becomes my effort?
What will I gain?
For the pain...
Will I face the shame or hold the ace?
I sought for the answer
I never got the answer.
It left me with fear.
I was scared.
I withdrew and never moved
I was stagnant and pretty shrewd.
When I realized it was all fear,
I wasn't really near
It was painful to bear

A lot of people have been captivated by fear
Believe me, it was never there.
Fear is fake.
Never make that mistake.
Be bold
Take the courage and lay hold.
Give it your all
Nothing is lost

Just an experience gained
It is never a break
If it breaks you
It will make you

Dear Wicked Employers
1/27/2018

Dear Wicked Employers
Who use employees like tyres
Then they fire and rehire
You change them like diapers
Your words are final
You bragged about sack letter
Then they start to panic
Due to unemployment statistics
They become static
And serve you like king
Bowing at your feet
No respect for their feelings
To you they are mess
You treat them like chess
You set unrealistic targets
They put their life on the line
They work till night
The love in their home decline

Home shattered
Children scattered
All you want is profit irrespective of the atmosphere
You forgot they aren't machine that has spare
They suffer pains they can't share
I have bad news for you
I will tell them the truth
And you will lose
Dear employees
Try see what's missing
Remember students spend three or five months per semester and pass their exams
How many months do an apprentice serve a master?

Six months or twelve and he becomes a master.
If you have served for ten years,
And still unhappy, start yours this year
Aren't you learning all this while
Why will you serve your whole life?

It's time to liberate
2018, you must elevate
Start to navigate
Success must circulate
Enough is enough
Like, comment and share
Wicked employers must disappear

Think About this Before You Take the Exit
By Itoto House Organization
2/2/2018

Think about this before you take the exit.

Walking away from that dream because of the obstacles.

You want to be great, but you don't want to fight your battle.

Don't be a fool!!.

You cannot always run when you should hold on.

Make the pain your fun.

A good wheel deserves another turn.

How do you see how good when you do not believe?

When have you already forfeited that big dream? What picture do you have in your memory?

The fear you will never achieve anything. That's the biggest lie anyone can tell you.

If you are telling yourself this, you are a fool.

Because they don't see the value in you, that should not stop you from doing what you are supposed to do.

You are the best motivation you can get Because you know yourself.

Where it hurts How it gets hot. You know a lot. Don't wait for anyone to carve a path they have not been through, your destiny is in your hands, so true. What will you do?

Stand up and face it, sounds cool. Say to yourself, I will come through!!!

"Become an active member today you will never lack support"

How Do I Face the Greatest Obstacle in My Way?
By Itoto House Organization
2/6/2018

How do I face the greatest obstacle in my way?
It has caused me stress and so much pains.
I have lost almost everything.
The courage to do the simplest thing is missing
Like I already presumed I am destined to fail
All my effort to no avail.
I become terrorized by the hurt
Inside me gets hot
I have learned a lot
But I still look lost.

Even the new month has started already,
And I am in great panic.
I need to talk to somebody
Maybe I will be relieved.
If this is your thought,
Read this and you will be taught.
Obstacles walk with success
Yes, it brings stress.
You have to give more not less
Else, you go on a recess
You have come far in life
You have done things you hate or like
If you aim high,
You must never stop to try.
You either try or sit and cry.
How big is that dream?
The obstacles are what makes it big
The stress is what makes it deserving.
Do not surrender to challenges,
Rather challenge all difficulties.

You are close to success
Don't look at the stress
Don't focus on the presence
What's the essence?
Nothing but to bring you down
To burn you out.
Will you give up?
It would have been better never to try than to stop.

I Have Finally Come to the End of the Road
By Itoto House Organization
2/7/2018

I have finally come to the end of the road.
I don't think I can overcome this battle have been fighting long ago.
Who said so?
How many times have you failed?
It doesn't matter the year, month or date.
A day of breakthrough eradicates hundred days of sorrow
So, don't let go.
Keep finding your own key to success
Don't die before death.
Don't deprive your health.
The world has a lot of problems to give you
Because they don't see the value in you,
That should not stop you from doing what you are supposed to do.
Just like a child writes exam at every level,
We do too.
Problems are testing time
Failures are part of success likewise
You will be left with one thing in the end,
The experience.
Soak it and be persistent
Be consistent and soon it will pay dividends
The earlier you know your own battle,
The better you are close to your breakthrough
Nothing is over
As long as you still have life, never say never.

Be the Solution NOT the Problem
By Itoto House Organization
2/13/2018

Suddenly you discovered you have stop growing.
Like you are a dead man living
You breathe, yes you do just like a living thing
But you discovered you are not really progressing
This is all you need to do
Look within yourself or look through
Everything starts with you
Where lies your treasure?
What have you been using to measure?

You could have all the certificate
If you don't know how to navigate,
If you don't know how to relate,
It might not pay

Will you spend all these years in school?
And still cannot even put food on your table

It sounds pathetic
Discouraging and depressing

All you need to do is find your hidden passion
Education gives you creativity to perform
Take an action
Join our team: https://itoto.org/register
sharing ideas on how to create solutions.
Find a problem
The world richest men are solving problems

Facebook, Twitter, Instagram, LinkedIn are solving the problem of networking, communication, etc.
Amazon is solving the problem of sales and marketing

Uber is solving the problem of transportation
All these are what you can do with your education
Solve the need of the people
It shows your true value

When you fold arms and dream,
Everyone does that too, only few pursue it
The more we dream without acting,
We are a dead man living
Stand up, find it, solve it and you will feel alive
The best feeling in life is having impact on lives
Regardless of what your calling might be have an impact on someone's life today: https://itoto.org/mentor/jobDescription

Do Not Add More to it... Enough Is Enough...
By Itoto House Organization
2/15/2018

Suddenly, I heard this voice
Like that of a boy
Deep inside me
From within

It told me: "your life has not been ruined."
You just need to rebuild
What have you lost?
Who have you mourned?
Are you lost on a path?
Or your strength has departed?
Do you think you can never be something good?
Or has the world turn you to a fool?
You don't even know what you want?
Let alone of knowing your worth?
You smile but deep inside you cry
You cried because you have tried
Every time but not worthwhile
You traveled many miles
But the destination was futile
You feel unlucky
With the journey
You toil every morning
Your neighbors see you as a workaholic
They envy you
Outside you look good
Inside you are not what they call you
In short, no value

WE ARE HERE TO SUPPORT YOU:
https://itoto.org/about

You thought of suicide
You are done with late night cry
You just want to leave this life
The life you chose
You were never close
Life instead, chose you
So, you felt life is a crook
What has life given you?
If it gives you shit, turn it to manure
Use it to grow your plants and watch it mature
If it gives what you have no interest,
Invest and you will see the interest.
Perhaps, invest your time, love, affection and interest
You may wait forever if you wait for what's perfect
Whatever life gives you is what you need to make life.
What you like may take your life.
If life gives you hate,
It is teaching you to rise above hate
It gives you disappointment,
It wants you to pick out your appointment
Not everyone will have it as they want,
But if we all reach out, we can get what we want.
Life is the best gift
Why do you complain about it?
Gratitude
Be grateful
Grateful you are still alive to complain
Only the living can feel pain
Is it the job?
It doesn't give joy
Try to be the source of your own joy
Nobody can steal it

Nothing can deprive you of having it
Once we understand life is like a road linking to other roads.
Now tell me, are the distance the same?
If no, why the complain?
Soak it
Love it
Cherish it
Don't add more to it

RATHER JOIN US TO HELP YOU SUCCEED: So Now WHAT'S Next??
By Itoto House Organization
2/18/2018

Trust you are good now...

Here's the post..

If you don't do it, someone else will do

If you don't do it, the world will not end

If you fail to move forward from the regrets, it is your own loss. No one's fault.

If you don't take the risk, the risk will take on you and you will be running all your life finding peace.

Whatever that doesn't come with a price, will make you a price. No free lunch in Freetown anymore.

It must take either monetary value or something else.

The easiest thing to do is to sit and cry or never try. You have nothing to lose but an opportunity that could turn your life around.

If you try, it is for your own good. Before you remember anyone else, you are always the first.

When things go wrong, look into the mirror first. There's always an answer for you.

Not all advice is good for you, every man speaks for himself and what works for him.

All success has a basis even though the paths might be different.

If you still dwell on regrets, you are living in the past.

This is a new week, take new opportunities and welcome new ideas.

Felix started mentoring freshmen from Africa in College at Edinboro University of Pennsylvania and Gannon University and gradually his efforts snowballed into a full-fledged student assistance program. Thus, Itoto House was born it was a part of Felix's project in the final year of his college. Today, the organization is growing globally and by the end of

2018, Felix is hopeful to be able to train/hire engagement representatives to grow further and reach out to more students.

Itoto House is geared to make international students bold and powerful so that they can bring out the best in them. The best part is that you will receive mentoring from people who have walked in your shoes earlier and are able to understand your situation from your perspective. We are building a sensible, knowledgeable and empathetic community where everyone will receive equal respective, regardless of location, culture, sex or race. We welcome you to a house where everybody is a member of a huge diverse family. We are looking forward to making the world a better place to live in.

It's Important to FREE Your Mind and Soul...
By Itoto House Organization
2/21/2018

Free your mind and soul
Let your spirit take control
Never lay hold,
Instead let go
The happiness that was borrowed
The joy that does not wait till tomorrow
They leave with a loophole
They make your destiny your foe
You cannot achieve your goal
They put your life on hold
I learned this long time ago
Nothing is like a joy behold
So, loosen up and unfold
Wish you can see, maybe you will follow
And never get cold
Flow with the flow
Life is not a party show
It is always you, your body and soul
If you think you have a backup, you are alone
You are on your own
So,
Be bold
Make courage your bow
Make action your arrow
Keep firing till you achieve your goals
There is always hope.

STOP.. LOOKING FOR SUPPORT
BE THE SUPPORT....
By Itoto House Organization
2/24/2018

Why should you do it?
If it brings you peace or profit.
How do you know when the time is right?
When you are not afraid to try.
Will you succeed if you do it?
No one knows when he will make it, just do it.

What if you fail?
As long as you are still alive, you will prevail.
Why does it seem impossible to do?
Because it is of no cheap value.
Why has everyone failed trying to do it?
That's enough motivation for you to break the jinx.
Do you think am strong enough to do it?
The richest man is not too full of muscle in him.
Do you think I have the brain?
If you still remember all that happened in your childhood, you have the brain.
What if no one supports me?
It is because you have not started it. People can't support an abstract thing.
How long will it take me?
It depends on how much you need it.
We have given you enough reasons to do that thing you have been contemplating?
If yes or no, let us know.

The Almighty Will Never Put You Through
What You Cannot Sustain or Survive.
By Itoto House Organization
2/26/2018

Living or dead?
Regress or progress?
Have you ever found yourself in a center?
You are not going forward either backward.
Just stagnant.
Do you take your career to the next level?
But you found yourself feeling regretful.
You regret making the move.
You wondered what is the next thing to do.
It wasn't clear to you.
I have been through it.
I moved to the United States as a foreign student.
Surviving was like a nightmare.
Majority of what the media depict was false
I felt all alone, lost, nervous, unwelcome, and Scared.
These any many other reasons prompted me to become a mentor.
Helping students who move abroad to study.
I want you to flourish
I want you to succeed.
It is difficult finding yourself in a strange land
Leaving your comfort zone
To achieve your goals
But it is not over.
You are not dead but alive
We will help the best way I can
This is just the beginning of empowering you
Be the first folks to have access to our upcoming book.
It is free. Procrastination will never get things done.
We rise by raising others.

Share with people who definitely need this.
Share with any student you know.

Be the first folks to have access to our upcoming book.
Be your brother's keeper.
God bless your endeavors
The Almighty will never put you through what you cannot sustain or survive.

Living or Dead?
By Itoto House Organization
2/26/2018

Regress or progress?
Have you ever found yourself in a center?
You are not going forward either backward.
Just stagnant.
Do you take your career to the next level?
But you found yourself feeling regretful.
You regret making the move.
You wondered what the next thing is to do.
It wasn't clear to you.
I have been through it.
I moved to the United States as a foreign student.
Surviving was like a nightmare.
Majority of what the media depict was false
I felt all alone, lost, nervous, unwelcome, and Scared.
These any many other reasons prompted me to become a mentor.
Helping students who move abroad to study.
I want you to flourish
I want you to succeed.
It is difficult finding yourself in a strange land
Leaving your comfort zone
To achieve your goals
But it is not over.
You are not dead but alive
We will help the best way I can
This is just the beginning of empowering you

Be the first folks to have access to our upcoming book.
It is free. Procrastination will never get things done.
We rise by raising others.
Share with people who definitely need this.

Share with any student you know.
Be the first folks to have access to our upcoming book.
Be your brother's keeper.

God bless your endeavors

Happy New Month March 2018
By Itoto House Organization
3/1/2018

March on from your problems.
March on from your temptation.
March on from your weaknesses.
March on from your instability
March on from your insecurity.
March on from your inability.
March on from poverty.
March on from your insincerity.
March on from your inferiority.
March on from your backward thinking.
March on from your anxiety.
March on from the unproductive.
March on from your disbelief.
March on from the guilt.
March from the evil society.
March on from your no value-added friends.
March on from being a victim.

March on from nothing to something.
Two months have gone, and why are you sitting?
Do you need magic?
It doesn't happen without a reason.
Look deep within.
Find the missing puzzle.
Adjust and blend with a new rhythm.
Don't continue with the old story.
Nothing is wrong with this World we are living.
You need to do something.
Happy New Month

Register at the link below to join our community:
Let's change the world together.
Please like comment and share.
Your word might but a smile on someone

IT'S NEVER TOO LATE!!!!!!! You Are NOT Alone
By Itoto House Organization
3/6/2018

It is obvious the grass is not always greener at the other side. You need to water the one at your side.

People tend to always relocate to find that place they can be great.

But is there really any place like that?

Can you sit back, think and answer that?

Do you think you have derailed from the track?

You looked back, all you could see is crack.

Nothing seems smooth to you. You wondered why you have made such move.

You have gone too far to go back.

You feel stuck like a child who just lost the mother in the crowd.

It leads to doubt. You wanted to opt out, but you felt you are on the lost side.

Don't worry. You are not alone. At Itoto house,

We can help you

√ leverage your skills

√ Develop your potentials

√ Make you feel at home even though you are a foreigner.

Kindly register at the link below

You Can Never Do it ALL Alone
By Felix Eshesimua
3/10/2018

Are you at a point in life?
You have walked many miles
Then you hit a crossroad
Then you are left all alone
A fall at that point will take you downfall
The roads are too good to follow
But you do not know which way to go
Too many subways
You are left with nothing to say
Nobody to talk to
Everyone is trying to figure out their own way too
Then you paused
You stayed too long
You looked back
You saw you have gone far
You look further
Doesn't shine brighter
You wished you were informed
Now you are feeling deformed
Regrets set in
You are fed up with soaking
What could be happening
You have no reason
What if there is a direction showing you the pathway
What if there's a voice telling you the way
I have been in a moment like this
Coming to study overseas
Hanging with the wrong crowd
been at the wrong place
I have no clue
I couldn't move

Then I was stuck
I almost stopped
I have come too far to go back
I looked up to faith and continued on the track
Somehow, I found success
I made progress
Now I want to give back
I want to help people get back on track
Are you lost?
Don't doubt your gut
At Itoto house, we help shape your career and put you in that area you need to develop your potentials
We a currently working on a success guide for you!

Sign up today, **https://itoto.org/register**
like and share with any student you know.
https://itoto.org/register

The Solution Starts Here
By Itoto House Organization
3/13/2018

The truth is
It was never missing
It was not far from reach
We just need a bit
A bit of hope
To reach out to our goal
Then focus on ourselves
Finding solution to the next
Next problem
Problem raising fear
Fear that held us for years
Years we could have achieved
Achieved the great things
Great things meant for us
But we couldn't
Now, is the time
Time to break away
Break away from the jinx
Break away from the curses.
We are lost
But now we are found
Order your step
Take the baby step
Reach out for help
In any way you need help
Like over here
We help foreign students
To find their feet
And succeed in their dreams
Join our team

I AM FOR YOU.. WORRY NO MORE..
By Felix Eshesimua
3/15/2018

We all must pay the price for living
No matter the reason
As long as we are breathing
Leaving my country to study was not easy
I left friends and family
Embarked on a journey
I have no clue what it will be
But I must leave
Sometimes life begins at the end of our comfort zone
Where we need to embrace hope
To achieve our goals
But always remember this
Whenever you want to give up on your dream
Reflect and think deep
Take this few hints
- life is meant to be lived
- nothing is easy
- we pay price to live
- breathe and breathe
- there is no guarantee
- just keep believing
My journey was never rosy
But I achieved my dreams
Been to sixteen countries
And still counting
I would love to help many international students out there
Who are stuck for years
And please share with any student you know

I Hate to Complain but this Has to CHANGE!!
By Felix Eshesimua
3/23/2018

I hardly complain unless I am getting paid to complain
I prefer to make a change
I do so by adding value to people's life
I struggled as an international student
Now am helping many international students out there
Some people don't understand that life has a price
It is sacrifice! Sacrifice!! Sacrifice!!!
When you sacrifice, never forget commitment.
To make your dreams come true; commitment, consistent and content
I call it the triple C
No magic
No get rich quick scheme
I am passing this message clearly
I don't want to offend anybody
If you feel offended, am sorry
Why is it majority of people that never struggle with you are the first to
come to you
I mean people who you called friends and family.
Who were the first you reached out to when things aren't going smoothly
Are the ones who turned their backs and gave excuses
But when they see you have built the foundation and making progress
They want to be part of the success
Don't show up when it starts to bubble
Don't waste your time giving reasons and excuses
When you were needed, where were you?
A stranger was here and committed
Saw the picture and now we have made progress
Indeed, failure is an orphan
Everybody has excuses

Everybody creates excuses
DON'T BE EVERYBODY!!
I will show you my Triple C formula.
It works!!

Fly Wide and Abroad
By Itoto House Organization
3/26/2018

I wish I could go back in years
So, I can overcome the fear
I wish I took that opportunity
I wish I never doubted my ability
I wish for this, I wish for that
This is the basic fact
No man is rich enough to buy the past
Let it go to move fast
Just like Marchem said, - *You alone can choose better*
Regrets do not solve matters, let it go
Else it becomes a load
It will drag you backward
When you should move forward
Failure means you tried to step up
Failure means try another method
Do not be bothered by what you should have done
Rather be concerned with how to make up for the wrongs
He who tries has a chance
The first sometimes could be the last
Embrace the shock
Never rely so much on luck
Rather put in hard work
Also, in this new world, network
Spread your wings across
Fly wide and abroad
Opportunities are everywhere
It is always near
You only need to connect to the right source
Solutions are never out of this world
Reach out when you are stuck
Learn to open your mouth and talk

It is wisdom to know when to ask for help
It is smartness knowing the next step
Ask yourself this question,
What next?
Have you taken a step and you are stuck?
No regret, we can help.
Our mission is helping international students finding their feet...
Do you know any?
Share the link below with them:
https://itoto.org/about

The Power of Gratitude
By Felix Eshesimua
3/30/2018

Gratitude for those who never believed in the dream
They made me see myself and channeled my energy on me
Gratitude to those who saw the Dream but failed to support
They made me invest all have got
Gratitude to those who badmouthed the result
No one is perfect, they forgot
Gratitude to those who disappeared along the journey
They made me trust my instincts
Gratitude to those who awaited my downfall,
They gave me more reasons to hold on
Gratitude to those who kept the faith,
They showed me I am great
Gratitude to the support from strangers
Sometimes strangers are better than brothers
Gratitude to the mentors who tutored me
Now I have achieved my dreams and growing big
Gratitude to my ups and downs
They made me see life is not for clowns
Gratitude to those who said I was weak
Now they all want to join the ship sailed by my team and I
Gratitude to the family who stood behind me
The support was solid and everlasting
Gratitude to those who contributed to the growth
Without you there would be no project called Itoto House (Powerful House)
Gratitude to those who await my first book
I promise to give you every clue you need to be successful

Gratitude for the support this month
As we move into next month,
I wish you

Joy
Happiness
New jobs
Settled home
Good partners
Promotion
And anything you ever wished for.
We help international students find their feet in their pursuit of fulfilment

What Is Your Plan?
By Felix Eshesimua
3/31/2018

Fulfillment!! Fulfillment!! Fulfillment!!
I can say I am fulfilled afterlife struggles
It was a hustle and bustle
Coming from another country and continent
To study in America as an international student
Friends you reached out for help, dejected
Even my project was neglected
It's all life
I try to live by
As a man, I cannot cry
I did jobs I was never meant to do
Sometimes at work I got screwed.
Life chose it
But I never accepted it
I decided to challenge it
A battle for freedom
It was cantankerous
I held on against the thorns
No doubt, it hurts
I bled within
I almost gave up and leave
But my family wanted me to succeed
If I go back,
I will be like a train lost on the track
That feeling when the whole family look up to you
So, you know you have to do what you are supposed to do
Anyway, I thank God
Who saw me through the odd

Then I set up a blueprint
To help international students find their feet
Just like mine who had climbed the hill
If you feel the same way, you can register with the link

5 Essential Tips for the New Month:
By Itoto House Organization
4/1/2018

This will definitely help you achieve your dreams. Life will not give you what you want but you can definitely create life from what it gives to you. How do you achieve that?

The Mind

The mind is like a driver. It propels your action. Anything we do, springs from the thought which is conceived from the mind. Possibility and impossibility are born in the mind. How sound is your mind?

Information

The quality of information the mind receives will determine the action taken. What type of information do you receive?

It's obvious we can't control what we hear but we can filter what we take in. Feed your mind with the right information and your mind will be productive.

Action

A thought remains a thought without action. A plan remains an abstract until a step is taken. You wonder why some projects couldn't get sponsors? Simple! No action was taken. Investors want to see a sign positivity before financing it. A little action taken is better than a well-documented idea.

Consistency

The ability to be reliable and dependable. The world is competitive. People are forgotten easily because everything is abundant. If we show up every day, or if we stick around for so long, it becomes difficult to ignore us.

No matter how good you are, if you lack consistency, it is like a mirage.

Time

Time is everything. Time is life. It is very expensive. Most people failed to realize and when they realized, it was late. No one is rich enough to go back in years.

If we can work with these five tips this month, there will definitely be a change. We help international students find their feet, kindly register with us.

Do People Really Care?
By Felix Eshesimua
4/5/2018

Get this straight
People don't care
Everyone has a lot to bear
Only few will be ready to hear
So, stop wasting your time to share
Stand up and grind!
There are no magic
Dream comes true from constant practice
Defeat comes with a reason
Failing to rise on your feet
Thinking you are not fit
Please, ignore it
Stand up and grind
Have you failed that success don't even know your name?
Even shame couldn't make you uncover your face
Inferiority complex couldn't make you relate
Why wait while time waste?
Stand up and grind
The road you travel is not straight
The curve even takes you off the way
You cannot navigate through the wave
It looks like you might soon break
Stand up and grind
The Storm is too strong
You are finding everything difficult
Your best seems not to be enough
You want to give up
After putting all
I can assure
You are more
You have more than enough

If only you can stand tall
Rise and grind
Lost in the desert
Couldn't find your path
In pursuit of your career
You have lost the track
You can't turn back
Neither can you move on
Just like a roundabout
Merry-go-round
Stand up and grind
Your dream is still achievable
Let's help you achieve it
Keep moving and keep pushing

Don't Give up on Yourself
By Itoto House Organization
4/8/2018

You wonder why that plan did not work
It is because you gave up
You gave up on yourself
You ran away from the test
Because it was too hard
All you wanted, you never had
You failed to try
Remember, life has a price
Every failure has a reason
Every champion stands every season
Life was not meant to be easy
If we understand this, it makes it easy.
Your destiny is in every opportunity
It comes like hard work for those discerning
Push for it
Push until something happens
Push until you get to your limit
Push with your energy
Trying is hard
Not trying is bad
Live your dream as long as you are living
Do the things while you still have the energy
Your good work saves you in the rainy days
It saves you from future shame
Push, never give up
Move on

Take Control of Your (Mind)
By Itoto House Organization
4/12/2018

We all know the mind is our driver
Like a chef, it cooks and serves the other parts
What your mind cook is what you do
Meaning all the actions spring from the mind
Ask yourself these questions:
what do you feed your mind with?
Positivity or negativity?
Take a rotten apple for example
You know you won't eat it because it is rotten
And harmful to your body and health
You know you will fall sick if you eat it
Same thing with your mind
Those negative thoughts are like rotten apples
They somehow harm you because it makes you do what you are not supposed to do
Instead, challenge your mind
Feed it with courage and see how things start to fall in line
Stay with the right people who will feed you with what is good
You are who you say you are
And that comes from what you think with your mind
Take a time to ponder and try to figure out
Those things that suck you up like bugs
That weigh you down and make you feel you cannot
It is time to let go
Free your mind and your soul
Take total control
As long as we are living, there's hope
You are the product of your thought
Start challenging it now
If you are an international student, you can join us using the link below:
https://itoto.org/register

Wisdom Is Knowing What You Don't Know
By Itoto House Organization
4/18/2018

Wisdom they say is the principle thing
So, you must get it by all means
Wisdom to right the wrong
Wisdom to live your life
Understanding tomorrow is full of hope
Believing the unknown
Wisdom to walk past the pain
And turn it to gain
Knowledge to see opportunity in adversity
Making profit from the hard thing
It requires wisdom to see the light at the end of the tunnel
After holding on in the toughest moment
What doesn't kill you makes you stronger
How would you have known if wisdom was not closer
You can't die before your time
Listen to that Wisdom voice: son you will be fine
He who lacks it suffers for the unknown
It is better than gold
Priceless to be sold
Wisdom is all I seek
To expand your career and discover your purpose in the land of the living
It is so sad it wasn't taught
Not even in the school of thought
But somehow,
You will always find wisdom

Hope this Can Keep You More Focus!! What New Skills Are Your Anticipating?
By Itoto House Organization
4/22/2018

What does the future hold for our beloved graduates?
With the alarming rate of unemployment in the world, do you still see people pursuing more academics certificates?

If yes, what does the future holds for our dear graduates?
Do you see education continuing?
A tough question but very simple to answer. Education will always be priceless. However, it is not a guarantee for success. It is a tool.
Having a tool doesn't mean you will be successful especially when you don't know what to do with it. Many graduates out there, only have mere certificates but cannot really apply it in the practical world.
Sometimes, I wonder if the current educational system is just breeding graduates who are dependent solely on the certificates. We seem to have more graduates who cannot think for themselves because of the mindset, 'I must get a job after graduation.'
After paying huge tuition to acquire certificates, why do graduates find it difficult to apply the knowledge acquired in the real world? The purpose of learning is to apply. If not, why learn it?.
As much as I know things are hard out there, but if you know better, you will surely do better. We are tired of breeding graduates who cannot add value to the world. They only want to take from the world. Life is a give and take principle.
Here are few points I will like to buttress:
- A certificate is not a guarantee for success
- It's better not to learn when you won't apply it
- Take away your certificate, what else can you create?
- Ensure you learn more skills, there is no crime in having additional knowledge
- Education is more than the four walls of an institution
We help international students find feet on the ground.

Connecting the Simple but Difficult Dots...
By Felix Eshesimua
4/25/2018

People often lament but at the end, they still take no step.

Can you grow with the unknown?

Many desire growth, but don't want to leave their comfort zone.

They want to pay nothing to get something

Not even a magician can do that.

If it was easy, everyone will have it.

It reminds me of the past, during my Master's

As an African,

I just came into America

I had big dreams. At some point, I almost leave to live. The bills became an uphill for me.

The more I nagged, the more things became hard

Till I start to embrace it, it was always difficult.

So, I decided to find out what went wrong.

I discovered I lacked three things:

Information

I wasn't well informed before embarking on the journey. I should have figured out the whole journey and the cost of living.

Mindset

My mindset wasn't built for survival. All I believed was I would get things at the snap of a finger. I was wrong.

Reliance

I was too reliant on people thinking I would get love in return. I was disappointed many times by so-called friends.

That's life. You must always think twice. Life is simple but only a few understood.

We help international students to find their feet on the ground. You can register at the link below

This Is Still Happening...In Most Developing Countries.
By Felix Eshesimua
4/27/2018

A person goes to school for free
With the aid of missionary
And support from the community
He builds his own school and makes it the most expensive
Not even the kids in his community could attend it
A celebrity raised by the community
Got big and exit from the locality
What's his reason for the exit?
He can't stay with the nonentity

A politician the masses voted in
Builds a big fence around his building
Goes about with security in sirens
Asking people to leave the road for him
You opened an account in the bank
You want to withdraw from the bank
The cashier sees a rich man in the stand
He asked you to move back
So, he can attend to the man
Preferential treatment becomes the order
A child you invested all your money
Becomes rich and won't attend a ceremony with mom
Because she's an illiterate, isn't that funny?
Friends you raised up
It's now hard for them to pick your calls
They said they need to catch up
Next time, we will talk
Companies we worked for
We clocked 50 and employers sacked us
Does age make a man know less or know more?
Advance technology,

Various communication techniques
New studies to improve human dealings
Communication is still broken
The problem of the world is human
Man and woman
Don't wait to change the world
Start with your neighbor
I am a product of the community
I lived all my life taking from the society
I want to give back with the right intentions
I want to serve international students all across the nation
To find your goal, you must first understand the scope and see if you can
cope.

Perhaps?
By Itoto House Organization
4/29/2018

Are you still owing yourself a debt?
I mean the debt of independence.
You feel you will not get there
Perhaps, you need someone's help
Of course, humans are dependent
But when it comes to what we want in life
It takes a bold step that is worthwhile
Every step is a step from where you are
Every mission starts with a decision
Every passion must go with an action
There's no flow without motion
A step further is a step closer
Are you still stuck?
Are you still dealing with the shocks of life?
It is time to be yourself
Stop living in pretense
Pay your debt by being the best you can be for yourself
Nothing satisfies a man than taking his stand
Remember, we are here for a purpose
Sometimes, it takes leaving the comfort zone
To achieve our goal
You may definitely find yourself alone
Never lose hope

Success Is in Sustainability
By Itoto House Organization
5/1/2018

You are successful when you have a successful successor.
Note:
As you build your company, think about the long run as well, when the going gets tough.

As you plan to acquire money, also, plan to invest. Wise people invest to make more interest while the rest save to spend.

As you look out for more clients or customers, likewise, plan to keep them. To keep clients, you must satisfy them.

As you plan for wedding, also plan for marriage. Wedding is just for a day, marriage is for a lifetime. Spend wisely.

As you build a house, build a home as well. House is a mere structure that could collapse. A home makes a house worth living.

As you secure a job, develop yourself. There's no job security anywhere. Every company wants more profit. So, you have to be on top of your game always.

As you build your skills, also, develop it to stay grounded. Skills can become obsolete leaving you in a tight corner. Explore and learn more.

Few remember yesterday, everyone is busy occupied by today…

If you work hard to get something, work harder to protect it. Because, you could build your company brand for years, and destroy it in a day.

The world itself is an ingrate. Be yourself, the universe will care of you only when you take care of yourself.
Happy prosperous month of May.

My New Names Are Love Trust Tolerance
By Felix Eshesimua
5/4/2018

Living the Life
I felt something went wrong in the world

Maybe not something, but all.
Even the seasons have changed
And places we used to visit in those days
Many dreams are buried
Goals are no longer achieved
Mission unaccomplished
People are not being nice
Everything is not fine
We don't even trust our neighbors
Despite all our efforts,
we still can't get enough comfort
Brother murders brother in a cold blood
What a weird world
A world meant to be simple
Became harmful
You can't even trust a friend
Let alone of doing business
Communication is broken
Homes are dismantled
Couples divorce
Many laws enforced
They say we are meant to be our brother's keeper
These days, we are our brother's haters
What went wrong?
What can be done?
The solution is her
You and I must be there
We must be the change

We must start bearing new names
The names are:

- Love
- Trust
- Tolerance

Then, we can have our beautiful world again.
Am tired of the pains and shame
Today, we are writing a new story
Are you an international student? Join us.
Together, let's build our dreams

Focus More on the Bigger Picture
By Itoto House Organization
5/7/2018

This new week:
Face your mountain and break it
Sail through your red sea to the shore
Run your race till you reach the last line
Be bold in your decisions and learn from any shortcoming
Up-level your game to stay ahead
Bury the past and move forward
Take it steady and focus on the important things
Quit nagging and do something
Change what you don't like rather than complain
Think twice before you decide
Treat everyone like you would love to be treated too

Be careful in what you say because it may backfire

Be careful who you trust because integrity is not a cheap thing

Believe in your dreams to achieve them
Believe in yourself to keep going against all odds
Speak out to be heard if you need help
Walk and work with great mindset to be orientated and motivated
Be original and be professional

Be Persistent
By Itoto House Organization
5/9/2018

Identify your weakness and focus more on your strength
You only know what is best for you

Remember, you can't be everything for them, else, you end up losing
yourself and they will definitely move to the next

It doesn't matter what you have done in the past, be consistent

It doesn't matter how many times you have failed, be persistent

Don't beat yourself too hard because of the mistake, no one is perfect

Don't be your own problem
Don't wait till everything is set, take a step
Start small but aim higher for yourself
Do it for your own interest,
It's nobody's business
We all have a life to live, so always learn
Life is not a contest
In the end, nothing is as sure as death
Do you want to spend all your life under another man's influence?
Living a life of pretense
I bet it, you will be lost like a shadow in the forest
I chose one thing, fulfilment
I breathe and be myself

When next I come into this world, I still choose to be myself

Go and be the best you owe yourself

Join us on the journey to greatness, join us with the link below

Shed it Off!
By Itoto House Organization
5/24/2018

Shed it off!

The load of worries

The hurt that has become a burden
The fear that has to limit you for years
The impatience that gives you the less
The ignorant that deprived you of something important
The anger that doesn't make you profit or give you peace
Unforgiving act...

It is more about us because our heart is always at stake.
The shackles that tie you from being free like the bird in the sky flying over the sea.
The guilt of your wrong deeds, yes, shed it off.
The relationship that steals your happiness and gives you sadness every day.

The friendships that add nothing to you except taking from you.
Being emotional when you ought to be professional
The past you have been battling to get over
Gripped by the mystery of the unseen future and it's killing your productivity
Yes, it is time to shed it off!

Won't you?
Why keep them?
Don't you want to be free?
Remember, the best thing in life is freedom.
It comes from living a world you want to see.

Making your own decision in a strong ocean
All these can only be attained if only you shed it off.
Yes, shed it off and be free.
Be part of a Global mission: **itoto.org/register**

International Student Success Stories

Name: Valdemar Reeves
country: Liberal
school: Edinboro University of PA USA
major: Business
career choice: Businesses Development
Bio: I'm Valdemar Reeves, an International Student from Liberia. A graduate from Edinboro University of Pennsylvania with a degree in Economics and Business Administration. I have a passion for Entrepreneurship and taking on the abilities of a Leader. I make it a huge part of seeing that the world is a better place for everyone.

Name: Placido Placide
Country: Uganda
School: Gannon University PA USA
Major: Master of Engineering
career choice: Software Engineer
Bio: Dedicated Software engineer my goal is to build and manage application that will help grow Uganda economy.

Name: Lotaya Nthabiseng
Country: Botswana
School: Coventry University United Kingdom
Major: Biomedical Science
career choice: Medicine
Bio: I am Biomedical Science student at Coventry University in England and I just recently completed the 1st year of my degree journey. I have lived in England for nearly 7 years. I am half South African, but I was raised in Botswana until 2011 where I moved here. I aim to give insight of life in the UK as an International student and also assist other international student to make their life as comfortable as I possibly can.

ABOUT THE AUTHOR

Felix Eshesimua

Felix Eshesimua, the Founder of Itoto House, was also an international student. He migrated to the U.S., from West Africa, to study at Edinboro University in Pennsylvania. Felix quickly learned that being an international student was a challenging endeavor that could easily derail the dreams of isolated students. Felix  founded Itoto House to provide a community of support and mentorship to help International students to achieve their fullest potential. Itoto means: I AM STRONG.

Connect with Felix at:
Facebook: https://www.facebook.com/felixspeak/
Twitter: https://twitter.com/felixeshesimua
Instagram: https://www.instagram.com/i_am_itoto/
Snapchat: @bossglobal
Website: http://www.felixeshesimua.com/
LinkedIn: https://www.linkedin.com/in/felix-eshesimua-mba-6a969a20/

Notes to Help You Connect with Itoto House for Support

Ask yourself the following questions. Use this section to make notes and have these notes ready when you connect with us at Itoto. This way we can do our best to help you achieve your goals, get the help you need, and help you to become one of our international student success stories.

What do you need coaching or mentoring with?

What are your biggest student needs at the moment?

What Itoto member benefits are you interested in, need, or would like to see available?

What are you studying and what are your plans after graduation?

Would you like to be a mentor to help other students?

What other thoughts, ideas, questions, etc. do you have after reading this book?

Coming Soon

A New Book from Itoto House

Financial Freedom for International Students

What you should do next:
Go to:
www.itoto.org/register
For Free!!

Printed in the United States
By Bookmasters